Signal Processing, Perceptual Coding and Watermarking of Digital Audio:

Advanced Technologies and Models

Xing He
SRS Labs Inc., USA

Information Science
REFERENCE

Senior Editorial Director:	Kristin Klinger
Director of Book Publications:	Julia Mosemann
Editorial Director:	Lindsay Johnston
Acquisitions Editor:	Erika Carter
Production Editor:	Sean Woznicki
Typesetters:	Milan Vracarich, Jr.
Print Coordinator:	Jamie Snavely
Cover Design:	Nick Newcomer

Published in the United States of America by
Information Science Reference (an imprint of IGI Global)
701 E. Chocolate Avenue
Hershey PA 17033
Tel: 717-533-8845
Fax: 717-533-8661
E-mail: cust@igi-global.com
Web site: http://www.igi-global.com

Library of Congress Cataloging-in-Publication Data

He, Xing.
  Signal processing, perceptual coding, and watermarking of digital audio: advanced technologies and models / by Xing He.
       p. cm.
  Includes bibliographical references and index.
  Summary: "This book focuses on watermarking, in which data is marked with hidden ownership information, as a promising solution to copyright protection issues and deals with understanding human perception processes and including them in effective psychoacoustic models"-- Provided by publisher.
  ISBN 978-1-61520-925-5 (hardcover) -- ISBN 978-1-61520-926-2 (ebook) -- ISBN 978-1-60960-790-6 (print & perpetual access) 1. Signal processing--Digital techniques. 2. Sound--Recording and reproducing--Digital techniques. 3. Sound recordings--Security measures. 4. Digital watermarking. I. Title.
  TK5102.9.H42 2012
  621.382'2--dc22
                                          2011003217

British Cataloguing in Publication Data
A Cataloguing in Publication record for this book is available from the British Library.

All work contributed to this book is new, previously-unpublished material. The views expressed in this book are those of the authors, but not necessarily of the publisher.

Dedication

To Mom, Dad and My Wife

Table of Contents

Preface

The availability of increased computational power and the proliferation of the Internet have facilitated the production and distribution of unauthorized copies of multimedia information. As a result, the problem of copyright protection has attracted the interest of the worldwide scientific and business communities. The most promising solution seems to be the watermarking process where the original data is marked with ownership information hidden in an imperceptible manner in the original signal. Compared to embedding watermarks into still images, hiding data in audio is much more challenging due to the extreme sensitivity of the human auditory system to changes in the audio signal. Understanding of the human perception processes and including them in effective psychoacoustic models is the key to successful watermarking. Aside from psychoacoustic modeling, synchronization is also an important component for a successful watermarking system. In order to recover the embedded watermark from the watermarked signal, the detector has to know the beginning location of the embedded watermark first.

In this book, we focus on those two issues. We propose a psychoacoustic model which is based on the discrete wavelet packet transform (DWPT). This model takes advantage of the flexibility of DWPT decomposition to closely approximate the critical bands and provides precise masking thresholds, resulting in increased extent of inaudible spectrum and reduction of sum to signal masking ratio (SSMR) compared to the existing competing techniques. The proposed psychoacoustic model has direct applications to digital perceptual audio coding as well as digital audio watermarking.

For digital perceptual audio coding, the greater extent of inaudible spectrum provided by the psychoacoustic model results more audio samples to be quantized to zero, leading to a decreased compression bit rate. The reduction of SSMR on the other hand, allows a coarser quantization step, which further cuts the necessary bits for audio representation in the audible spectrum areas. In other words, the audio compressed with the proposed digital perceptual codec achieves better subjective quality than an existing coding standard when operating at the same information rate, which is proven by the subjective listening test.

Digital audio watermarking applications will benefit from the proposed psychoacoustic model from two perspectives: a) It can embed more watermarks to the inaudible spectrum, which results to a watermark payload increase and b) It hiding higher energy watermarks to the audible spectrum areas possible, which leads to improved robustness and greater resiliency to attacks and signal transformations than existing techniques, as proven by the experimental results.

We finally introduce a fast and robust synchronization algorithm for watermarking which exploits the consistency of the signal energy distribution under varying transformation conditions and uses a matched filter approach in a fast search for determining the precise watermark location. The proposed synchronization method achieves error free sample-to-sample synchronization under different attacks and signal transformations and shows very high robustness to severe malicious time scaling manipulation.

Chapter 1
Introduction of Human Auditory System and Psychoacoustics

This chapter reviews the background of human auditory system (HAS) and psycho-acoustics.

1.1 SIMPLE INTRODUCTION OF THE EAR

The ear consists of three separate parts, the outer, middle, and inner ears as shown in Figure 1 (Wikipedia, 2009).

The outer ear consists of the head, the pinna, and the external auditory canal. The main function of the pinna is to locate the source of the sound, especially at high frequencies. Auditory canal is where the sound travels through to hit the tympanic membrane. The outer ear offers frequency directivity by shadowing, shaping and diffraction. Different people localize sound differently due to considerable

DOI: 10.4018/978-1-61520-925-5.ch001

Figure 1. Diagram of the ear

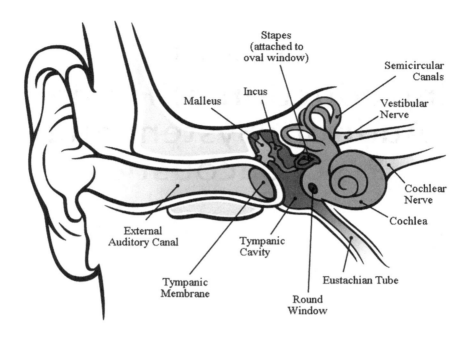

variations in the pinna. A generalized summary of such ability for average listener is modeled by the "Head Related Transfer Functions" (HRTF's) or "Head Related Impulse Responses" (HRIR's).

The air-filled middle ear is composed of the eardrum (tympanic membrane), the opening of the eustachian tube and the 3 small bones (ossicles), including the malleus (hammer), incus (anvil) and stapes (stirrup) (Bharitkar, et al. 2006). The sound vibrations in the ear canal are transmitted to the tympanic membrane, which causes movement of the malleus, incus and stapes. Then stapes footplate pushes on the oval window, causing the movement of the fluid within the cochlea in inner ear. Here the whole ossicles act as an amplifier, transmitting the sound vibrations and passing them through to the fluid-filled inner ear.

The inner ear is constituted of the cochlea, containing the organ of corti, two membranes (basilar membrane and tectoral membrane) and the associated fluids and spaces (Bharitkar, et al. 2006). The cochlea is lined with tiny hair cells, which create nerve signals when the sound reaches cochlea.

1.2 PROPERTIES OF THE HUMAN AUDITORY SYSTEM

Psychoacoustic modeling is important in audio coding and watermarking to ensure changes to the original signal remain imperceptible. Compared to the human visual system (HVS), the HAS is much more sensitive, which makes the audio watermarking more challenging than image watermarking (Cox et al., 2002). The HAS can detect signal with a range of frequency greater than 10^3:1 and with power greater than 10^9:1 (Painter et al., 2000). Understanding how the HAS perceives sound important for the development of a successful audio watermarking system.

Although exact models of the HAS do not exist today, great progress has been made in the field of psychoacoustics to model human auditory perception as well as the time-frequency analysis capabilities of inner ear. The main property of audio perception lies in the masking phenomena which includes pre masking and post masking (explained later in section 1.4). Another issue in audio perception is the absolute threshold of hearing which is illustrated as follows.

1.2.1 Absolute Threshold of Hearing

In psychoacoustics the intensity of a sound is measured in terms of Sound Pressure Level (SPL). The SPL gives the level of sound pressure in decibels (dB) in reference to the internationally defined reference level $p_0 = \mu Pa$, or $2 \times 10^{-5} N / m^2$ (Newton per square meters), which corresponds to the threshold of audibility at 1000 Hz. This level is given by $SPL = 20 \log_{10}(p / p_0)$ dB, where SPL is the measured Sound Pressure Level, p is the sound pressure of the stimulus reaching the ear, in Pascals [Newton per square meters (N/m^2)] (Spanias, et al. 2007).

While the HAS is highly sensitive compared to HVS, it has its own limits. The HAS cannot perceive the sound if its SPL is below some threshold. Such threshold is called absolute threshold of hearing, which determines the energy for a pure tone that can be detected by the HAS in noiseless environment. The absolute threshold of hearing is a non-linear function varies according to the audio frequency and can be approximated by

$$T(f) = 3.64(f / 1000)^{-0.8} - 6.5e^{-0.6(f/1000-3.3)^2} + 10^{-3}(f / 1000)^4 (dB)\ SPL \qquad (1.1)$$

and it is depicted in Figure 2 (Painter et al., 2000)

In Figure 2 (Zwicker et al., 1990), we can see that the HAS is most sensitive to the audio with frequency range around 2 kHz to 5 kHz and not sensitive to audio

Figure 2. The absolute threshold of hearing

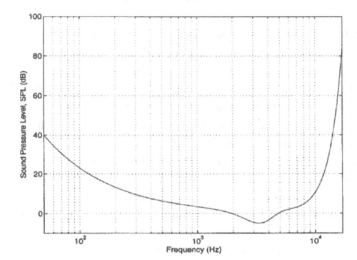

with frequency greater than 10 kHz. The area below the absolute threshold of hearing is called the quiet zone and the audio signal that falls into quiet zone is not perceptible.

1.2.2 Critical Bands

In the presence of an acoustic stimulus the basilar membrane in the human inner ear performs a short-time spatio-spectral analysis on the incoming sound. This process is done in specific overlapping regions of the basilar membrane (Deller et al., 1993). Experiments showed that human sensitivity to acoustic events is related to the unevenly spaced frequency scale. The term "critical band" describes regions of equivalent sensitivity in this frequency scale and is defined as the frequency band within which the loudness of a band of continuously distributed sound of constant SPL is independent of its bandwidth (Atal et al., 1984). The critical band is rated on the so-called *Bark* scale. Because the critical bands are unevenly spaced, the "Bark" scale is a nonlinear frequency scale (Deller et al., 1993). The cycles-per-second (Hz) to Bark mapping is described by the following formula:

$$z = 13 \arctan(0.76 \frac{f}{1000}) + 3.5 \arctan(\frac{f}{1000})^2. \tag{1.2}$$

Figure 3. Cycles-per-second to bark mapping

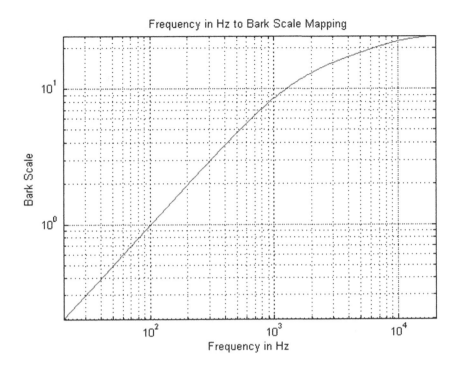

where f is in Hz and z is in Bark. Barks are rounded to the nearest integer to provide the *critical band index*. Figure 3 illustrates such mapping.

The critical bandwidth at each center frequency is closely approximated by

$$BW_c(f) = 25 + 75(1 + 1.4(\frac{f}{1000})^2)^{0.69} \tag{1.3}$$

The critical bands and its bandwidth is listed in Table 1 (Zwicker et al., 1991) and shown in Figure 4.

Although critical bands notation is widely used in psychoacoustic modeling and perceptual audio coding, there is an alternative called equivalent rectangular bandwidth (ERB), which models human hearings as brick rectangular band pass filters and provides an approximation to the bandwidths of those filters.

To convert a frequency in Hz to a frequency in units of ERB-bands, the following formula should be used, namely

Table 1. Standard critical bands distribution

Critical Band Index	Lower Edge (Hz)	Center Edge (Hz)	Upper Edge (Hz)
1	0	50	100
2	100	150	200
3	200	250	300
4	300	350	400
5	400	450	500
6	510	570	630
7	630	700	770
8	770	840	920
9	920	1000	1080
10	1080	1170	1270
11	1270	1370	1480
12	1480	1600	1720
13	1720	1850	2000
14	2000	2150	2320
15	2320	2500	2700
16	2700	2900	3150
17	3150	3400	3700
18	3700	4000	4400
19	4400	4800	5300
20	5300	5800	6400
21	6400	7000	7700
22	7700	8500	9500
23	9500	10500	12000
24	12000	13500	15500
25	15500	19500	

$$ERB_c(f) = 21.4 \log(4.37 \frac{f}{1000} + 1) \tag{1.4}$$

Figure 5 shows this conversion.

The bandwidth of an ERB filter centered at a given frequency f is

$$BW_{ERB}(f) = 24.7(4.37 \frac{f}{1000} + 1) \tag{1.5}$$

It is important to note that the formula above converts a frequency (in Hz) to a bandwidth (also in Hz), which is illustrated in Figure 6.

1.3 THE MASKING PHENOMENA

Auditory masking refers to the phenomenon where one sound becomes inaudible due to the existence of another sound. The sound being masked is called maskee

Figure 4. Critical bandwidth at each center frequency

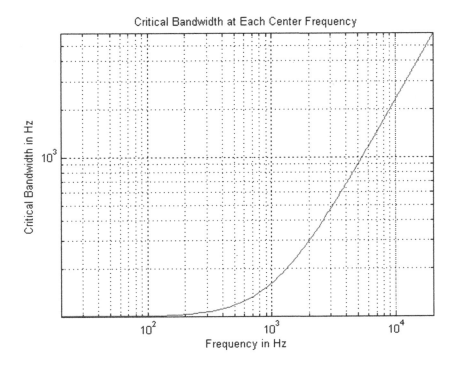

and the sound that masks the other sound is called masker. There are two types of auditory masking phenomena: simultaneous masking and non-simultaneous masking, which are also referred to as frequency masking and temporal masking.

1.3.1 Simultaneous Masking

Standard critical bands distribution (Table 1) happens when two or more sounds are present at the same time and the weaker signal is rendered imperceptible because of the presence of the stronger signal, in another words, the weaker signal is masked by the stronger signal. Whenever there is a stimuli, it creates a masking threshold and makes inaudible any signal that falls below the masking curve. Figure 7 (Zwicker et al., 1990) shows the masking thresholds of five pure tones at 0.07 kHz, 0.25 kHz, 1 kHz, 4 kHz and 8 kHz. The broken line is the absolute threshold of hearing.

There are many types of simultaneous masking and the mainly three simplified paradigms of simultaneous masking are noise-masking-tone(NMT) (Scharf, 1970), tone-masking-noise(TMN) (Hellman, 1972), and noise-masking-noise(NMN) (Akansu, et al. 1996).

Figure 5. Frequency in Hz to ERB bands conversion

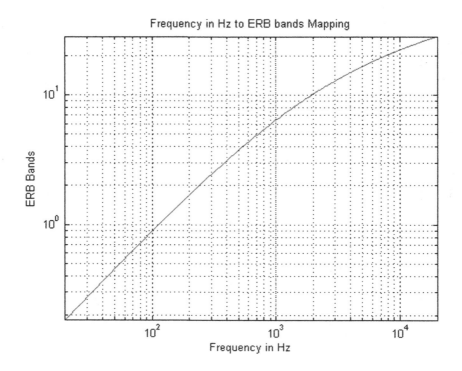

In the noise-masking-tone scenario, a narrow band noise with bandwidth of 1 Bark masks the tone within the same critical band, when the intensity of the tone is below certain dB of the intensity of the masking noise. The difference of the intensity between the maker (noise) and the maskee (tone) is called the signal masking ratio (SMR), which becomes the smallest when the frequency of the tone is close to the center frequency of the noise. Typically, the SMR for noise masking tone is about 4 to 5 dB, which means when the tone signal has intensity 4 or 5 dB less than the intensity of the noise in the same critical band, the tone will become inaudible. An example is illustrated in Figure 8 where a 410 Hz pure tone with 76 dB SPL (sound pressure level) is rendered inaudible by the band limited noise centered at 410 Hz with 80 dB SPL (Spanias, et al. 2007).

The tone masking noise case, on the other hand, is the phenomena where the noise signal becomes inaudible or masked by the excitation of a tone signal in the same critical band. Studies showed that the general minimal SMR for a tone to mask noise is about 21 to 28 dB. Figure 9 shows an example of tone masking noise case where the 1 Bark narrow band noise centered at 1 kHz is masked by a 1 kHz pure

Figure 6. ERB bandwidth at a given frequency

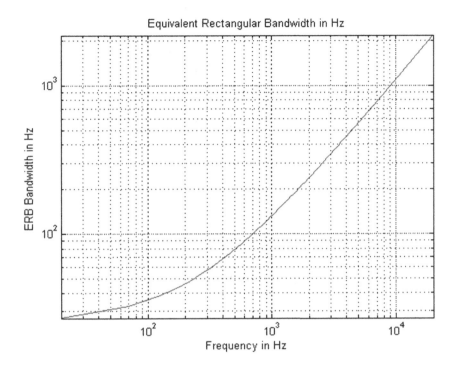

Figure 7. Frequency masking thresholds of pure tones at 0.07 kHz, 0.25 kHz, 1 kHz, 4 kHz and 8 kHz

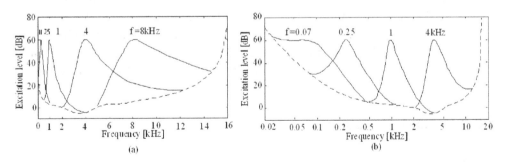

tone, note however, the intensity of the noise is 24 dB less than that of the tone (Spanias, et al. 2007).

In the noise masking noise scenario, a narrow band noise is masked by another narrow band noise. One study showed that wide band noises can produce about 26 dB SMR in the noise masking noise case.

Figure 8. Noise masking tone example

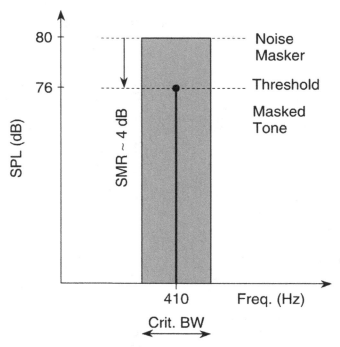

1.3.2 Asymmetry of Masking

As it can be easily seen from Figure 9 and Figure 10, noise is much more effective as masker, creating much higher SMR compared to tone signal. It is easy for narrow band noise to render a tone signal in the same critical band inaudible with barely 4 dB SMR. However, in order to mask the narrow band noise at the same critical band, a tone signal has to have the intensity 21 to 28 dB higher than that of the noise signal.

1.3.3 Spread of Masking

An excitation signal can not only create simultaneous masking effect and render other weaker audio signal in the same critical band inaudible, but can also create such masking effect across nearly critical bands. This phenomenon is called the spread of masking.

This effect is often approximately modeled by a triangular spreading function with slopes of 25 and 10 dB per Bark. A general formula of such approximation can be expressed as (Painter et al., 2000)

Figure 9. Tone masking noise example

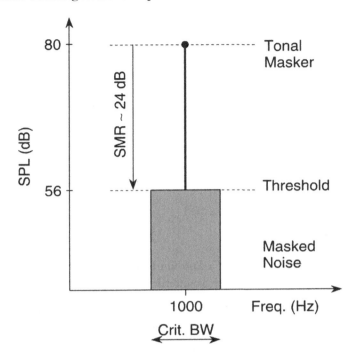

$$SF_{db}(x) =$$
$$15.81 + 7.5(x + 0.474) - 17.5\sqrt{1 + (x + 0.474)^2}$$

(1.6)

Where *x* has units of barks an has units of dB.

1.4 TEMPORAL MASKING

A strong stimuli can not only generate simultaneous masking, but also create masking effects even before its onset or after its present. Such masking phenomenon is called non-simultaneous masking or temporal masking. The masking phenomenon before a sound onset is called pre-masking and the one after its presence is called post-masking.

Figure 10 (Painter et al., 2000) illustrates the non-simultaneous masking property of the HAS. Note that although pre-masking lasts only several milliseconds, post-masking can last up to 200 milliseconds.

Figure 10. Temporal masking property of the HAS

REFERENCES

Akansu, A., & Smith, M. J. T. (1996). *Subband and wavelet transforms, design and applications*. Norwell, MA: Kluwer Academic Publishers.

Atal, B., & Schroeder, M. R. (1984). Stochastic coding of speech signals at very low bit rates. In *Proceedings of the IEEE International Conference on Communications* (pp. 1610-1613). Amsterdam, Netherlands.

Bharitkar, S., & Kyriakakis, C. (2006). *Immersive audio signal processing*. New York, NY: Springer. doi:10.1007/0-387-28503-2

Cox, I. J., Miller, M. L., & Bloom, J. A. (2002). *Digital watermarking*. San Francisco, CA: Academic Press.

Deller, J. Hansen, J., & Proakis, J. (1993). *Discrete-time processing of speech signals*. New York, NY: Macmillan Publishing.

Hellman, R. (1972). Asymmetry of masking between noise and tone. *Perception & Psychophysics, 11*, 241–246. doi:10.3758/BF03206257

Painter, T., & Spanias, A. (2000). Perceptual coding of digital audio. *Proceedings of the IEEE, 88*(4), 451–513. doi:10.1109/5.842996

Scharf, B. (1970). Critical Bands. In Tobia, J. V. (Ed.), *Foundations of modern auditory theory,* (1, pp. 157-202). New York, NY: Academic Press.

Spanias, A., Painter, T., & Atti, V. (2007). *Audio signal processing and coding*. Hoboken, NJ: Wiley-Interscience Press. doi:10.1002/0470041978

Wikipedia (2009). Retrieved from http://en.wikipedia.org/wiki/Ear

Zwicker, E., & Fastl, H. (1990). *Psychoacoustics Facts and Models*. New York, NY: Springer-Verlag.

Zwicker, E., & Zwicker, U. (1991). Audio engineering and psychoacoustics: matching signals to the final receiver, the human auditory system. *Journal of the Audio Engineering Society. Audio Engineering Society, 39*, 115–126.

Chapter 2
Introduction of Digital Watermarking

2.1 MOTIVATION AND GOALS

The increase in computational power and the proliferation of the Internet has facilitated the production and distribution of unauthorized copies of multimedia information. As a result, the problem of copyright protection has attracted the interest of the worldwide scientific and the business communities. The most promising solution seems to be the watermarking process where the original data is marked with ownership information hidden in an imperceptible manner in the original signal. Understanding of the human perception processes is the key to successful watermarking. Typical properties of a successful watermarking scheme includes (Cox et al., 2002)

a.   The watermark should introduce no perceptual distortion.
b.   The watermark should be embedded into the host signal, rather than into an added header of that signal.

DOI: 10.4018/978-1-61520-925-5.ch002

c.   The watermark should be hard to remove, or even detect without the prior knowledge of the watermarking scheme and the watermark sequence.

d.   The watermark should be self-clocking, which also know as synchronization problem.

e.   The watermark should be readily extracted to completely characterize the copyright owner.

The motivation of this book is to exploit the fundamental issues of digital watermarking and provide new solutions. We focus our research on the most important two key components of a watermarking system, namely psychoacoustic modeling and perfect synchronization. The former component makes the embedded watermarks inaudible while the latter makes recovery of embedded watermarks possible.

2.2 WATERMARK APPLICATIONS

The applications of digital watermarking include but not limited to broadcast monitoring, owner identification, proof of ownership, transaction tracking, content authentication, copy control and device control (Cox et al., 2002).

2.2.1. Broadcast Monitoring

Some organizations and individuals like advertisers, performers and owners of copyrighted works are interested in broadcast monitoring. For advertisers, they want to make sure that they receive all the air time they paid for radio/TV station. For performers, they would like to collect the royalties from radio or TV stations when broadcasting their works. For owners of copyrighted works, they want to make sure their works are not illegally re-broadcasted by other unauthorized stations.

Although they could have a human to monitor the broadcast by watching, listening or recording the broadcast, it is expensive and error prone. Watermarks however, can be embedded to the content before broadcasting. Computer systems can then be used to monitor broadcasting by detecting the existence of watermarks from the broadcasted content.

2.2.2. Owner Identification

Copyright information on an image is usually printed on the original work by a texture copyright notice, which could be aesthetically unattractive and may cover a portion of the image. For other media like music, such copyright information can only be displayed on the physical media (CD, tape), which makes the owner identification hard to maintain when audio is transmitted over the internet. Watermark technology could be used to embed such owner identification into media files imperceptibly before the works get distributed. The watermarks should be robust enough to survive the channel noise, possible signal processing and even malicious attacks. For the audio case, the distributed audio file may undergo compression / de-compression, up or down sampling, AD / DA conversion. The copyright information embedded by watermarks can still identify the ownership after those possible processing.

2.2.3. Proof of Ownership

Watermarks can be used not only to identify ownership, but also to prove the ownership. Consider the following scenario Alice is the owner of one piece of work. Before distributing the work into the market, she embeds her ownership information into the work to identify her ownership. Bob is an adversary and after he gets the watermarked work, he embeds his own copyright information as watermarks into the work and claims the ownership of the work. Now, how can Alice prove her ownership of the work? The solution lies in embedding a highly secure watermark, which prevents unauthorized watermark embedding, detection or removal.

2.2.4. Transaction Tracking

Another application of watermarking is transaction tracking where a unique watermark is embedded into each copy of the work before distribution. Such watermark contains the unique information of the buyer of each copy. If some buyers make illegal copies and sell them to pirate producers, the watermark that contains the buyers' information can be extracted from those bootlegs thus the owner can identify the buyer who was responsible for the leakage.

2.2.5. Content Authentication

In some scenarios the sender may want to make sure that the work does not get modified during transmission and the receiver receives the original work. Fragile watermarks are used in this situation to make content authentication possible. One or more fragile watermarks are embedded into the work before sending it out. The receiver will first try to detect and extract those fragile watermarks and see if any changes have been made to the work during transmission. If the work undergoes any modifications, even the slightest ones, those fragile watermarks will disappear. In another words, if the receiver can successfully detect and extract those watermarks, he or she knows the piece of work received is authentic without any added modifications.

2.2.6. Copy Control

Instead of detecting wrongdoings done to copyrighted media, copy control aims at preventing people from doing wrongs. Take the illegal copy of DVD or CD disk for instance, a watermark meaning "No Copy" could be embedded into each copy of the media before distribution. The recording device, meanwhile, has a watermark detector integrated that can detect the "No Copy" watermark. Such recorder will refuse to make the copy of those copyrighted media which has "No Copy" watermark.

2.2.7. Device Control

Synchronization and control watermarks may be embedded into radio and TV signals. An example is the Dolby FM noise reduction technology used by some radio stations to reduce the noise in the broadcasted music. The watermarks embedded in radio signal will trigger the Dolby decoder in the radio, thus providing better quality music.

Several techniques in audio watermarking system have been developed in the past decade including lowest-bit coding, phase coding, echo coding, spread spectrum, quantization index modification (QIM), (Bender et al., 1996). Chapter 4 provides a literature review of the current state-of-the-art audio watermarking techniques and Chapter 1 already illustrated the background of psychoacoustic models, which are important for audio watermarking. In this chapter, we will only take a look at the overall picture of a typical watermarking system.

2.3 ELEMENTS OF A WATERMARKING SYSTEM

A typical watermarking system is illustrated in Figure 1. The secret message m (watermark) is embedded into the host signal s with a secret key k and the watermarked signal w is represented by

$$w = f(m, k, s) \tag{2.1}$$

where f is the watermarking function.

The watermarked signal (stego-signal) is then transmitted over the channel to the receiver and the signal may get distorted due to possible channel noise. The distorted signal at receiver side is denoted as

Figure 1. Typical watermarking system

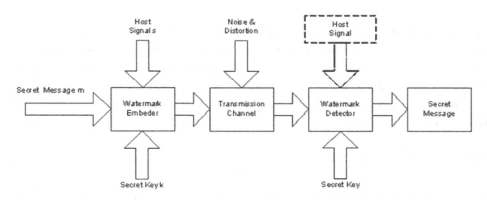

$$\hat{w} = w + n \tag{2.2}$$

where *n* is the channel noise.

The watermark detector performs two sub functions: watermark decoding and watermark detection.

The watermark decoding function decodes the received watermark $\hat{m}$ using the secret key *k* and it determines whether the host signal is watermarked by the secret key k based on the recovered watermark.

There are two types of detectors: informed detector, where the host signal is available during decoding phase and blind detector, which has no access to the host signal.

2.4 ORGANIZATION OF THE REST OF THE BOOK

The rest of the book is organized as follows:

Chapter 3 illustrates new applications of digital watermarking, including a) error detection, concealment and recovery; b) quality of service in multimedia communications or subject and subjective signal quality measurement; c) bandwidth extension; d) security of air traffic control or secrete communication. Chapter 4 gives the background and literature review of selected watermarking techniques. Due to the dominant popularity of spread spectrum used in digital watermarking, Chapter 5 through Chapter 7 will focus exclusively on this technology. Chapter 5 presents the principles of spread spectrum. Chapter 6 reviews the survey of current audio watermarking schemes based on spread spectrum. Chapter 7 proposes several techniques to improve traditional spread spectrum detection. Chapter 8 introduces our proposed discrete wavelet packet transforms (DWPT) based psychoacoustic model, which takes advantage of the flexibility of DWPT decomposition to closely mimic the critical bands, thus providing precise masking thresholds. Chapter 9 proposes a high quality perceptual audio coding method using the psychoacoustic model from Chapter 8. Experimental results show that the proposed audio codec outperforms the widely used MPEG I Layer III (MP3) method by providing better audio quality. Chapter 10 describes an improved spread spectrum watermarking system using the psychoacoustic model from chapter 8. This watermarking system achieves better robustness compared to the main methods based on perceptual entropy (PE) psychoacoustic model. Chapter 11 proposes an enhanced watermarking system based on the system in Chapter 10. The enhanced system achieves higher robustness, more security and faster decoding process compared to the previous system. Chapter 12 deals with the synchronization problem. Here, we introduce a fast and robust synchronization algorithm for watermarking by exploring the stability of high energy distribution, utilizing a matched filter for the precise localization. Chapter 13 summarizes the book and gives future research trend in digital watermarking.

REFERENCES

Bender, W., Gruhl, D., Morimoto, N., & Lu, A. (1996). Techniques for data hiding. *IBM Systems Journal*, *35*(3/4), 313–336. doi:10.1147/sj.353.0313

Cox, I. J., Miller, M. L., & Bloom, J. A. (2002). *Digital watermarking*. San Francisco, CA: Academic Press.

Chapter 3
Novel Applications of Digital Watermarking

The introduction chapter has presented the copyright related applications of digital watermarking include but not limited to broadcast monitoring, owner identification, proof of ownership, transaction tracking, content authentication, copy control and device control (Cox et al., 2002). This chapter will focus on not so typical watermark applications namely non-copyright related applications including:

a.   Error Detection, Concealment and Recovery
b.   Quality of Service In Multimedia Communications
c.   Subject and Subjective Signal Quality Measurement
d.   Bandwidth Extension
e.   Security / Air Traffic Control / Secrete Communication

DOI: 10.4018/978-1-61520-925-5.ch003

Figure 1. General error detection, concealment and recovery communication system

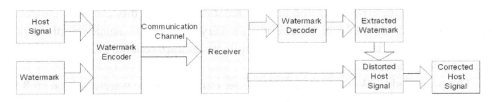

3.1 ERROR DETECTION, CONCEALMENT AND RECOVERY

A general diagram of error detection, concealment and recovery communication system using watermarking is illustrated in Figure 1.

The watermark, which carries characteristics information of host signal, is embedded into host signal with watermark encoder in an un-intrusive way so that the introduced watermark is not perceivable. After being transmitted through the noise communication, the signal reached at the receiver is a distorted host signal. The watermark is extracted by the watermark decoder from the contaminated signal. This watermark then is used to help recover the host signal by correcting or concealing the errors.

Packet loss or delay usually occurs when transmitting multimedia in wireless and Internet environment. Protocols like UDP and TCP either leads to partial representation or requires re-transmission, which introduces intolerable time delay.

Lin et al. (2001) proposed an error detection and concealment in UDP environment using self-authentication-and-recovery images (SARI). Watermarks which contain content based authentication and recovery information are embedded into SARI image or video frames prior to transmission. At the receiver side, the embedded authentication information in the watermark is used to detect the locations of corrupted image blocks and the recovery information is employed to approximately restore the lost blocks.

The embedded watermarks are claimed to be compatible with quantization–based lossy compression like JPEG / MPEG. Since the watermarks are embedded prior to transmission, no extra control over the transmission or encoding process is needed. At the receiver side, the recovery is not based on adjacent image / video blocks, thus making it possible to restore packet loss in large areas or high variant areas.

Chen et al. (2005) proposed a fragile watermark error detection and localization scheme called "force even watermarking" (FEW) for wireless video communications, where compressed video streams are extremely sensitive to bit errors including random and burst bit errors, which hinder correct playing of the steaming video. In the proposed FEW algorithm, a fragile watermark is forcedly embedded on the DCT coefficients at the encoder side. During the decoding process, the same watermark is checked first for error detection and the locations of error bits can be accurately localized at macro block level. Since error recovery methods are usually employed at MB level, the localization ability of this fragile watermark scheme greatly improves the success of conceal erroneous MBs.

The proposed FEW watermarking encoder embeds fragile watermark on an 8 x 8 DCT macro block by forcing certain DCT coefficients quantized to even values, i.e. all the 64 quantized DCT coefficients after the typical zigzag scan position are rounded to the nearby smaller even values. This embedding procedure happens right after the normal video encoding quantization process. At the decoder side, if any of the received DCT coefficients in 8 x 8 block has odd value, then the system knows errors have occurred to that block during transmission.

According to their experimental results, compared to the traditional syntax-based error detection schemes, the proposed FEW scheme doubles the error detection probability, greatly improves the correctly locating an error by 3 to 13 times and yields a low image degradation of less than 0.44 dB.

Transmitting block-coded images through wireless channels, which is error-prone, usually results high packet losses. Gür et al. (2007) invented an error concealment algorithm to provide a close approximation of the lost packets, thus covering up the packet losses.

In their algorithm, replicas of the host image's M x M macro blocks in the subbands with two wavelet schemes namely wavelet-tree and pyramid-structured wavelet LL subbands are left untouched to limit the visual degradation. In order to achieve blind detection, a shared-key-dependent pseudo-random sequence (PN sequence) is used to choose the host macro blocks where watermarks (replicas in this case) are inserted.

The watermark encoder works as follows:

The original image is first divided into M x M macro blocks and the macro blocks with all 0's are chosen. One pixel value in each of the chosen macro blocks are replaced with value 1, acting as a fragile watermark for error detection. is used to store the scaled watermarks / replicas is generated by storing each $M / 2^k$ by $M / 2^k$ macro block of the tree structured DWT (Discrete Wavelet Transforms), where k is the number of levels of such DWT. Designed coefficients are used to scale those replicas, which are embedded into the subbands of lth level pyramid-structured DWT of the host image chosen by the shared key dependent PN sequence, excluding LL subbands. Inverse DWT (IDWT) is applied on the above image to get the final watermarked image.

At the decoder side, the fragile watermark in the all "0" macro blocks is first checked for lost blocks. l^{th} level pyramid-structured DWT is applied on the received

Figure 2. General watermarking multimedia QoS evaluation system

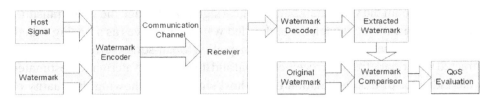

image and the locations of the replicas of lost macro blocks are located by the shared-key dependent PN sequence used in encoder. k^{th} level IDWT are applied after the extracted replicas multiplied by the scaling coefficients shared with encoder. The average of all non-zero extracted macro blocks are used to approximate the lost macro block. The image after this process is called extracted image. If there are still lost macro blocks in the extracted image, then median value of the neighboring macro blocks are use to replace the lost macro blocks. The final image is called healed image.

In their experiments, the received image has been seriously damaged with 50% loss of macro blocks. Using the proposed method, the authors successfully healed the image and greatly improved the perceptual quality of the distorted image.

3.2 QUALITY OF SERVICE IN MULTIMEDIA COMMUNICATIONS

Besides copyright protection purpose, researchers also proposed employing watermarking techniques for testing quality of service (QoS) in multimedia communications.

A general diagram of such QoS evaluation system using watermarking is illustrated in Figure 2.

The watermark, which is usually fragile, is embedded into host signal with watermark encoder transparently. After being transmitted through the noise communication, the signal reached at the receiver is a distorted host signal. The watermark is extracted by the watermark decoder from the contaminated signal. Since the watermark and the host signal undergo the same noise channel, the damage made to the host signal quality should have the same effect on the watermark quality. By compare the differences / errors between the extracted watermark and the original watermark, the QoS of the multimedia communication system can be estimated / evaluated.

Campisi et al. (2002,2003) introduced a blind quality assessment system for multimedia communications using tracing watermarking. In their presented method, a fragile watermark is embedded into host video stream with spread spectrum technology. Since both the watermarks and the host signal go through the same transmission / communication channel, the embedded watermark serves as a tracing signal, dynamically evaluating the communication quality. Mean-square-error between the extracted watermark from the received signal and the original watermark is estimated as the indicator of the degradation of the host signal, thus showing the quality of multimedia communication system. The proposed method could be used in applications like evaluation of quality of service (QoS) of wireless communication systems, like the mobile Universal Mobile Telecommunications System (UMTS) services.

Benedetto et al. (2007) proposed a method for QoS assessment of 3G video-phone calls by tracing watermarking exploiting the new color space 'YST'.

In the typical video calls, although both voice and MPEG-4 video images (usually the caller's face in the foreground) are transmitted, the faces of the speakers are generally the most important region of interest in the communication, which makes the skin color important for still images. Therefore, in order to minimize the perceptual distortions introduced by digital watermarking, the authors presented a novel color space based on the 'skin' component.

In the new defined color space, i.e. YST, the luminance component is the same of YUV while the S (skin) component is estimated as the average values of a set of different colors of people's faces. The T component is defined as orthogonal to the YS plane.

The assumption of this watermarking based QoS evaluation is that the distortion suffered by the embedded watermark are likely suffered by the host data since they are transmitted through the same communication channel.

In order to mitigate /eliminate noticeable distortion introduced by the embedded watermarks, spatial spread spectrum technology is used to spread the narrow-band watermarks over much larger bandwidth host image so that watermark energy is negligible small for each host frequency bin.

A pseudo-random noise (PN) matrix is used to spread the watermark, which is then attenuated by a watermark strength factor and added back to the original image in discrete cosine transform (DCT) domain, as in the following equation

$$Y_i[k_1, k_2] = X_i[k_1, k_2] + \alpha w_i[k_1, k_2] \qquad (3.1)$$

Where $w_i[k_1, k_2]$ is the watermarked *ith* frame of the image in DCT domain, $X_i[k_1, k_2] = DCT(x_i[k_1, k_2])$ is the DCT of *ith* frame of original image, $w_i[k_1, k_2] = w[k_1, k_2] * p_i[k_1, k_2]$ is the *ith* frame of spread watermark and $w[k_1, k_2]$ is the original watermark, $p_i[k_1, k_2]$ is the *ith* frame of PN matrix, $[k_1, k_2]$ is the

Figure 3. General subject speech quality measurement system using watermarking

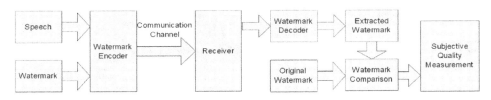

index according to mid-high frequencies of the image. a is watermark strength factor employed to balance the tradeoff between the evident of watermark and the degradation of the image quality.

The watermarking processed signal is then transmitted through the communication channel where the signal might suffer from noise and other distortions. At the receiver side, the watermark decoder extracts the watermark, compares it with the original watermark and evaluates the QoS by computing its mean-square-error (MSE) as an index of the degradation level.

By updating the QoS estimates, the wireless multimedia communications can control feedbacks to the sending user on things like link diagnostics; quality monitoring and QoS based billing.

3.3 SUBJECTIVE SIGNAL QUALITY MEASUREMENT

A general diagram of subject speech quality measurement system using watermarking is illustrated in Figure 3.

Similar to previous application, the quality of speech signal can be subjectively measured by checking the quality of the extracted watermark from the received signal.

Cai, et al. (2007) proposed a novel speech quality evaluation method by using digital watermarking. In the traditional way, speech quality is evaluated with subjective tests, which is very expensive and time consuming and not applicable for applications like online monitoring. Objective tests, which usually require the original reference speech or complicated computation model, are not applicable for some speech quality evaluations. The proposed method evaluates the speech quality without such constrains (requires no reference speech or complicated computation model) by embedding watermarks in discrete wavelet domain or temporal domain of a speech signal with quantization technology. Various speech distortions caused by Gaussian noise, MP3 compression, low pass filtering and packet loss could be

Figure 4. General bandwidth extension system using watermarking

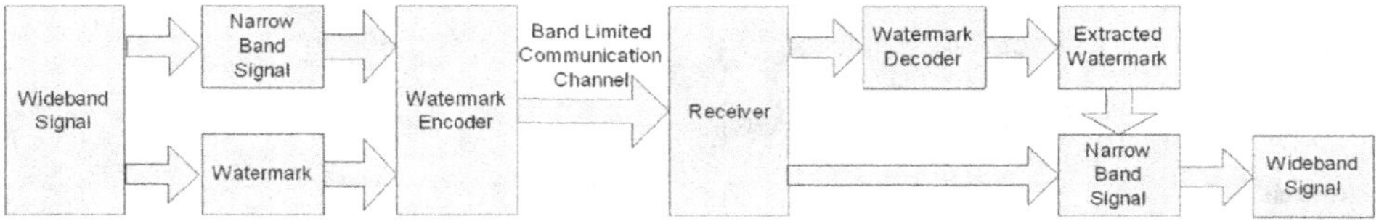

accurately evaluated as compared to the results of perceptual evaluation of speech quality (PESQ).

The proposed speech quality evaluation system consists of three components: watermark embedding, watermark extraction and speech quality evaluation.

In order to mitigate the impact on signal quality distortion introduced by watermarking, a quantization based method with optimized adaptive scale to a speech signal is employed for both watermark embedding and extraction. Watermarks are embedded in discrete wavelet transform (DWT) coefficients of the speech signal if speech quality is evaluated after speech being MP3 compressed; low pass filtered and Gaussian noise polluted. If however, speech quality is to be evaluated after speech signal passed packet loss communication channel, then the watermarks are embedded in temporal domain. The same algorithm is used for speech quality evaluation component. Under the assumption that the embedded watermarks undergo the same channel distortion as the host speech, percentage of correctly extracted watermark (PCEW) is computed as an indicator of the degradation of speech quality.

3.4 BANDWIDTH EXTENSION

Bandwidth extension is another new area that watermarking can play an important role.

A general diagram of bandwidth extension system using watermarking is illustrated in Figure 3.4

The embedded watermarks typically are parameters reflecting the higher band information of the original wideband signal. Those information are used to reconstruct the wideband signal at the receiver side.

Geiser et al. (2005) introduced an artificial bandwidth extension of speech supported by watermark-transmitted side information, which is based on estimating parameters of speech production model. The wideband speech communication networks, which offer better speech quality and intelligibility by transmitting 7 kHz or higher bandwidth speech signal, typically use wideband speech codec such as the adaptive multi-rate wideband (AMR-WB). However, such system is hard to be compatible with current standardized narrowband equipment which can only handle speech signal with less than 4 kHz bandwidth. In order to satisfy the backward compatibility in narrowband communication systems, the side information, which is used to support the parameter estimation, is embedded into the narrowband speech as digital watermark.

Geiser et al. (2007) further developed the above method and presented a code-excited linear prediction (CELP) watermarking and bandwidth extension based backwards compatible wideband telephony in mobile networks. In previous watermarking method, the watermarks are embedded into the speech signal before the coding, which makes the watermark bits severely suffered when the speech signal being coded by CELP codecs (GSM Enhanced Full Rate (EFR) for example). Extra error concealment / recovery have to be employed to extract the embedded watermark. The new proposed watermarking algorithm integrates the watermark embedding into the CELP speech codec, thus solving the above mentioned issue. With typical watermarking scheme, the watermarks are embedded into less or least relevant components of the speech signal to avoid perceptible distortion. Those less or least relevant components, however, are also most likely coarsely quantized or omitted by speech coders, which makes the watermark extraction unreliable. The proposed watermarking scheme takes account into the CELP coder's specific characteristics so that the embedded information will not degrade the perceptual quality of the speech signal while maintain robustness. Due to those considerations, pulse positions are chosen to embed the watermarks. According to the experimental results, when operating at narrowband mode, the proposed method achieves the same mean opinion score (MOS) compared to EFR codec. At wideband mode, the proposed EFR_WB coder when operating at 12.2 kbits/s with 400 bit/s of hidden side-information for high band synthesis, achieves similar speech quality comparing to G.729.1 codec at 14 kbis/s and AMR-WB codec at 12.65 kbits/s.

Sagi et al. (2007) also proposed a bandwidth extension method for telephone speech aided by data embedding. The narrowband speech signal is used as carrier to carry the bandwidth extension information, which is embedded as watermark. The high frequency of the wideband signal is reconstructed at the receiver side with the embedded side information. More specifically, two components are used for the high frequency band reconstruction, a synthetic wideband excitation signal, generated directly from the base band speech, and a wideband spectral envelope, whose parameters are transmitted by the hidden data.

In the encoder side, the signal is first transformed to frequency domain and partitioned into subbands with discrete Hartley transform (DHT). Psychoacoustic model is computed within each subband to choose the appropriate DHT coefficients for modification. The parameters of the upper band are embedded into those chosen modified DHT coefficients in a way that is transparent to the listeners with the

Figure 5. General improved ATC security system using watermarking

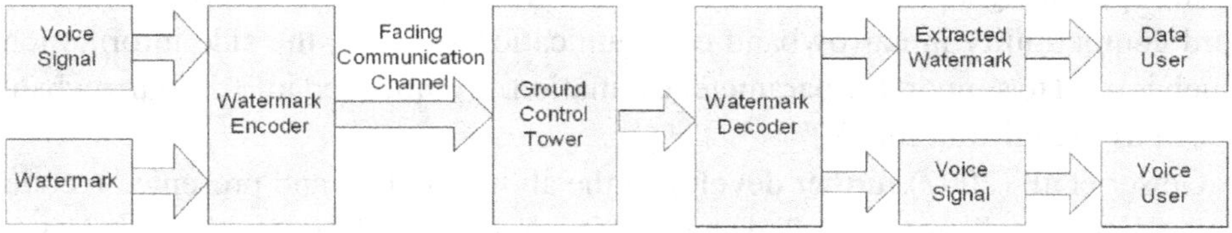

guide of the computed auditory masking thresholds. According to their claim, the proposed scheme achieves 600 bits/s watermark embedding rate when transmitting over a typical telephone line with a bit error rate of approximately 0.03%. The reconstructed wideband speech is preferred 92.5% over the traditional telephone signal in their conducted listening test.

3.5 SECURITY / AIR TRAFFIC CONTROL / SECRET COMMUNICATION

Other security related applications for watermarking have also been proposed by researchers, including increasing the safety of air traffic control (ATC) voice communications by using in-band messaging, speech watermarking for air traffic control and speech watermarking for the VHF radio channel,

A typical diagram of improved ATC security system using watermarking is illustrated in Figure 5.

The watermarks are typically authentication related identification numbers like user ID or aircraft ID, which is embedded into the voice signal as speech watermarks. The watermark encoder is usually integrated with the Push-to-Talk (PTT) system. Ground controller receives the watermarked voice through very high frequency (VHF) fading audio channel. Watermark decoder is used to extract the watermark and recover the original voice signal. The watermark is sent to data user for authentication.

Sajatovic et al. (2003) presented a novel idea to increase the safety of the ATC voice communications by embedding in-band messages. In their design, a new "digital" feature- aeronautical messaging service is added to the traditional analog radio telephony (R/T) system to increase the ATC safety. Although digital voice systems have been introduced to the communication systems, they require major changes to the currently widely used analog voice systems, which most of the ATC communications are based upon. During the ATC communications, the pilots and controllers within the same sector use PTT to access the same R/T communication channel. This voice system, although applicable to current ATC communications, has some significant drawbacks, including not supporting user identification and addressing at the system level. Those information have to be exchanged between pilots and controllers via voice at the beginning of the communication. Possible misunderstanding (confused user ID, for instance) between pilots and controllers during those analog voice based communication process over the noise radio transmission fading channel could lead to serious safety risks. A new concept called data in voice (DiV) is raised by the authors to solve such issue by offering methods for user identification and authentication of the user of the R/T channel. Part of the audio frequency (AF) spectrum (2040 Hz to 2340 Hz) is replaced by a narrow-band modem signal to convey the in band message, which can provide fast enough data rate (up to 240 bits/s) to broadcast a short data message (user ID, for example) at the beginning of each R/T communication event. On the ground controller side, the received signal is fed in parallel into a band-reject filter and an in-band modem. The output of the band-reject filter is the voice forwarded to the voice user and the output of the in-band modem is the DiV message sent to the data user.

They also mentioned other potential applications of the proposed DiV concept including a) talker identification, where information like aircraft call sign is transmitted along with pilot's voice to control towers with each PTT event; b) secure voice application, where the receiver can authenticate the sender of the in-band message with a "security envelope" created by DiV system.

Hagmüller et al. (2005) proposed a similar idea to enhance ATC security by transmitting additional hidden aircraft identification data with voice communications over the VHF channel between pilots and controllers. Those additional hidden information are embedded in the voice as speech watermarks in a perceptually transparent way. Spread spectrum technology is employed in the watermarking system to spread the watermark over a much wider frequency spectrum so that each frequency bin only contains very low watermark energy, thus keeping the embedded watermark below audible level.

A sophisticated linear prediction model for watermark spectral shaping is included in the watermark embedding process to further prevent the possible perceptual distortions introduced by watermarking.

BCH-code, which can both detect and correct errors, is used for error control. The system can transmit watermarks at 12 bits/s with hardly audible distortion and less than 0.01% very low error rate. For higher watermarking rate, the system can reach 24 and 36 bits/s watermarking rate with slightly audible distortion and low error rate.

Hofbauer et al. (2005) further summarized speech watermarking for the VHF radio channel including system elements, watermarking methods.

As they mentioned in the paper, the system elements include a) voice signal; b) watermark; c) watermark encoder; d) transmission channel; e) received signal and f) watermark decoder. The typical watermarking technologies include a) multi-tone sequence; b) data-in-voice (DiV); c) spread spectrum; d) informed embedding; d) speech parameter-based watermarking and e) speech perception based watermarking.

They also pointed out it is important to develop a mathematic model of the voice channel of a VHF radio including a) radio transmitter and receiver and b) transmission channel. Moreover, they proposed a method to measure time-variant impulse responses of the aeronautic VHF radio channel between a fixed or moving aircraft and a ground-based control tower.

REFERENCES

Benedetto, F., Giunta, G., & Neri, A. (2007). QoS assessment of 3G video-phone calls by tracing watermarking exploiting the new colour space 'YST'. *IET Communications*, *1*(4), 696–704. doi:10.1049/iet-com:20060331

Cai, L., Tu, R., Zhao, J., & Mao, Y. (2007). Speech quality evaluation: a new application of digital watermarking. *IEEE Transactions on Instrumentation and Measurement*, *56*(1), 45–55. doi:10.1109/TIM.2006.887773

Campisi, P., Carli, M., Giunta, G., & Neri, A. (2002). Tracing watermarking for multimedia communication quality assessment. In []. New York, NY.]. *Proceedings of the IEEE International Conference on Communications*, *2*, 1154–1158.

Campisi, P., Carli, M., Giunta, G., & Neri, A. (2003). Blind quality assessment system for multimedia communications using tracing watermarking. *IEEE Transactions on Signal Processing*, *51*(4), 996–1002. doi:10.1109/TSP.2003.809381

Chen, M., He, Y., & Lagendijk, R. L. (2005). A fragile watermark error detection scheme for wireless video communications. *IEEE Transactions on Multimedia*, *7*(2), 201–211. doi:10.1109/TMM.2005.843367

Cox, I. J., Miller, M. L., & Bloom, J. A. (2002). *Digital watermarking*. San Francisco, CA: Academic Press.

Geiser, B., Jax, P., & Vary, P. (2005). Artificial bandwidth extension of speech supported by watermark-transmitted side information. In *Proceedings of the 9th European Conference on Speech Communication and Technology* (pp. 1497-1500). Lisbon, Portugal.

Geiser, B., & Vary, P. (2007). Backwards compatible wideband telephony in mobile networks: CELP watermarking and bandwidth extension. In *Proceedings of the IEEE International Conference on Acoustics, Speech and Signal Processing (ICASSP)* (4, pp. 533-536). Honolulu, HI.

Gür, G., Altug, Y., Anarim, E., & Alagöz, F. (2007). Image error concealment using watermarking with subbands for wireless channels. *IEEE Communications Letters, 11*(2), 179–181. doi:10.1109/LCOMM.2007.061055

Hagmüller, M., & Kubin, G. (2005). *Speech watermarking for air traffic control. EEC Note 05/05*. Eurocontrol Experimental Centre.

Hofbauer, K., Hering, H., & Kübin, G. (2005). Speech watermarking for the VHF radio channel. In *Proceeding of the 4th EUROCONTROL Innovative Research Workshop* (pp. 215-220). Bretigny, France.

Lin, C., Sow, D., & Chang, S. (2001). Using self-authentication-and-recovery images for error concealment in wireless environments. []. Denver, CO.]. *Proceedings of the Society for Photo-Instrumentation Engineers, 4518*, 267–274.

Sagi, A., & Malah, D. (2007). Bandwidth extension of telephone speech aided by data embedding. *EURASIP Journal on Advances in Signal Processing*. doi:10.1155/2007/64921

Sajatovic, M., Prinz, J., & Kroepfl, A. (2003). Increasing the safety of the ATC voice communications by using in-band messaging. In *Proceedings of the 22nd Digital Avionics Systems Conference* (1, pp. 4.E.1-1-8). Indianapolis, IN.

Chapter 4
Literature Review of Selected Watermarking Schemes

This chapter gives a review of selected state-of-the-art watermarking techniques that are widely used in watermarking systems.

4.1 LSB CODING

One of the earliest attempts of information hiding and watermarking for digital audio signal is least significant bit (LSB) coding / replacement. In the simplest implementation, the least significant bit of the host signal is replaced by the to-be-hidden watermark bit. In a more secure scenario, the watermark encoder uses a secret key to choose a pseudo random subset of the all of the host signal samples. The replacement of watermark is performed on those chosen samples. In the decoder side, the same secrete key is used to select those watermarked bits in the received signal.

DOI: 10.4018/978-1-61520-925-5.ch004

In order to recover the whole watermark, the decoder needs all the stego samples used by the encoder. The obvious advantage of LSB is the high watermark capacity. For example, when using only the least significant bit of the CD quality (44.1 kHz sampling rate, 16 bits per sample) host signal, the encoder can achieve 44,100 bits per second (bps) watermark capacity. Some audio watermarking system uses the least 3 or even 4 significant bits of the host audio signal for watermarking embedding, achieving super high 132.3 kbps to 176.4 kbps watermark capacity. Another advantage of LSB coding is the simplicity, which requires very little computation cost for both the watermark encoder and decoder, making real time watermark embedding and extraction possible, even for computation power limited devices. However, although it's simple to implement, LSB has several disadvantages:

a.   The random replacing of the samples selected by the encoder introduces low energy additive white Gaussian noise (AWGN), which is very perceptible to human auditory system (HAS), creating annoying audible distortion.
b.   LSB coding has very little robustness. Simple attack like random cropping or shuffling will destroy the coded watermark.
c.   The depth of LSB is limited. In order to minimize the possible audible distortion, only the least 4 significant bits of the 16 bits per sample host audio signal can be used for watermark coding purpose.

4.2 PATCH WORK

Patch work was originally developed for image watermarking (Bender et al. 1996) and later being used for audio watermarking as well. Patch work algorithm uses statistical hypothesis on two sets of large samples for information hiding, which makes it a good method for audio watermarking due to the huge amount of digital samples in audio host signal. In the simple patch work encoding scenario, a secrete key is used to pseudo randomly select two sets of samples, i.e. patches. The amplitude of each sets are slightly changed in the opposite way, i.e. the amplitude of one set samples are increased by a small amount d and the amplitude of the other set samples are decreased by the same amount. d is carefully chosen according to the following rules:

a.   It is not too small so that it is robust to possible added noise during transmission and
b.   It is not too large to introduce audible distortion.

This can be illustrated in as:

$$a_i^w = a_i + d$$
$$b_i^w = b_i - d$$

(4.1)

Where a_i and b_i are the ith sample of the randomly selected two sets A and B, respectively. a_i^w and b_i^w are the same samples after slight value modification (watermarking process).

At the decoder side, the same secret key is employed to choose the same two sets of data. Then the difference of the expectation of those two data sets is computed. If it equals to *2d*, the stego signal is watermarked. This process goes as follows:

$$E\left(A - B\right) =$$
$$\frac{1}{N}\sum_{i=1}^{N}(a_i^w - b_i^w) = 2d + \frac{1}{N}\sum_{i=1}^{N}(a_i - b_{i)})$$

(4.2)

Due to the random selection of large data sets, the last portion of the equation is expected to be zero, so

$$E\left(A - B\right) = 2d$$

(4.3)

The problem for patch work is that in the real application system, the mean difference between two randomly selected data sets is not always zero. Although the distribution of the mean difference of those two watermarked patches is shifted to the right of the unwatermarked version by 2d, there is still some overlap between the two distributions as illustrated in Figure 1. Therefore, there lies probability of wrong detection. Increasing the amount of modification *d* will make the detection more accurate with the higher risk of introducing possible auditable distortion.

4.3 QUANTIZATION INDEX MODULATION

The quantization index modulation (QIM) is another popular watermarking scheme that hides information by quantizing samples. The maximum value of the input sample is found to determine the quantization step d. Each sample is then quantized with the determined quantization step. A slight modification is then made to each quantized sample according to the watermark. In (Kim, 2003), the author introduced

Figure 1. Patch work watermarked vs. unwatermarked distribution

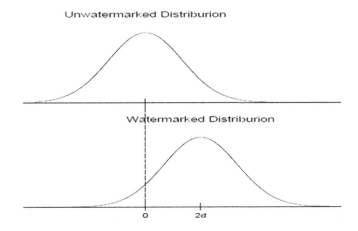

a simple implementation of QIM as follows: suppose the input host sample is x, the quantization step is d, the quantization function is q(x,d), the watermark bit to be embedded is w (0 or 1), then the watermarked sample y is denoted as:

$$y = q\left(x,d\right) + \frac{d}{4} * \left(2 * w - 1\right) \tag{4.4}$$

The quantization function is defined as:

$$q\left(x,d\right) = \left[\frac{x}{d}\right] * d \tag{4.5}$$

where [x] is the rounding function which rounds to the nearest integer of x.

In Figure 2, the sample x is first quantized to the q(x,d) or black circle. If the to be embedded watermark bit is 1, then the d/4 is added to the quantized sample value which moves the sample up to the while circle. Otherwise, d/4 is removed from the quantized sample value, which moves the sample down to the cross (x).

At the decoder side, the difference between the received sample and its quantized value is computed. If it is between (0,d/4), then the extracted watermark bit is "1". If the difference lies between (-d/4, 0), then the embedded watermark bit is "0". Otherwise, the received signal is not watermarked. This can be illustrated with following equations:

Figure 2. QIM illustration

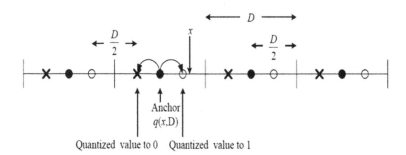

Quantized value to 0   Quantized value to 1

Suppose the received signal is y, embedded watermark bit is w, quantization step is d, then

$$w = 1, if \, 0 < y - q\left(y, d\right) =< \frac{d}{4} \tag{4.6}$$

$$w = 0, if \, -\frac{d}{4} =< y - q\left(y, d\right) < 0 \tag{4.7}$$

The author also gave a simple example for the quantization modulation method in the same paper. Suppose the value of the input sample is 81, the quantization step d is 8, then when watermark bit "1" is embedded, the value of the sample becomes:

$$y1 = q\left(81, 8\right) + \frac{8}{4} = 82 \tag{4.8}$$

When watermark bit "0" is embedded, the value changes to:

$$y0 = q\left(81, 8\right) - \frac{8}{4} = 78 \tag{4.9}$$

At the decoder side:

$$y1 - q\left(y1, 8\right) = 2 \tag{4.10}$$

so the extracted watermark bit is "1"

On the other hand

$$y0 - q\big(y0, 8\big) = -2 \tag{4.11}$$

so the extracted watermark bit is "0"

QIM is very simple to implement and it is robustness to slight noise addition attack. As long as the noise introduced at transmission channel is less than d/4, the detector can always correctly extract the watermark. If, however, the noise exceeds d/4, the watermark might not be precisely detected. This is a tradeoff between watermark robustness and transparency. A larger quantization step d will be more robust against jitter with the risk of creating audible distortion to the host audio signal.

4.4 ECHO CODING / HIDING

Echo coding / hiding embeds data into a host audio signal by introducing an echo. The offset (or delay) between the original and the echo is so small that the echo is perceived as added resonance. The four major parameters of this method are: initial amplitude, decay rate, "one" offset and "zero" offset (illustrated in Figure 3). (Bender et al., 1996; Gruhl et al., 1996)

Figure 4 shows the echo kernels used in a typical echo hiding scheme. "1" and "0" are using different kernels which have different offset. A typical echo example is shown in Figure 5 (Gruhl et al., 1996).

Figure 6 shows the encoding process of echo hiding (Gruhl et al., 1996). The original signal is mixed with "one" kernel or "zero" kernel according to the watermark content and thus producing the encoded signal.

In the decoding process, the space between the echo and the original signal is detected and the embedded watermark is extracted according to the space. In order to do this, we have to examine the magnitude of the autocorrelation of the encoded signal's cepstrum at two locations (Bender et al., 1996).

$$F^{-1}(\ln_{complex}\big(F(x)\big)^2) \tag{4.12}$$

where F represents the Fourier Transform, F^{-1} the inverse Fourier Transform. In each segment the peak of the auto-cepstrum detects the embedded binary data.

Echo hiding embeds data into a host audio signal by introducing an echo. The nature of the echo is to add resonance to the host audio and not to make embedding

Figure 3. Adjustable parameters

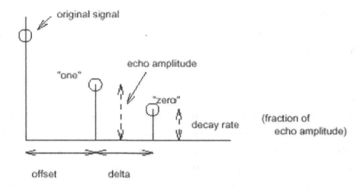

signal as additive noise. It is possible to embed the signal to audio while having the same statistical and perceptual characteristics. Meanwhile, echo hiding provides many benefits from various points of view including robustness, imperceptibility, simple encoding, decoding process.

But robust watermarking requires high energy echo to be embedded which increases audible distortion. So, there is a tradeoff between inaudibility and robustness.

Bender et al.(1996) proposed the stereotype of echo hiding in 1996. The original model used a single positive echo to hide one bit of information ("one" or "zero") and the whole system achieved 16 bps of data payload. But the robustness of this system is weak and it is easy to do echo detection by malicious attacks.

Figure 4. Echo kernels

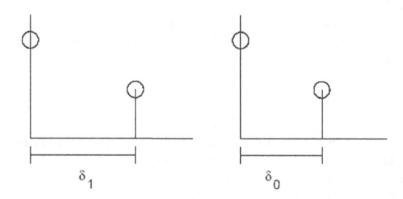

Figure 5. Echo examples

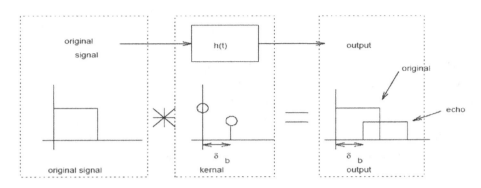

Xu et al. (1999) proposed a multi-echo embedding technique. Instead of embedding one large echo into an audio segment four smaller echoes with different offsets were chosen. The amplitude of echoes can be reduced due to multiple echoes. This may reduce the possibility of echo detection by third parties because they do not know the parameters. But the technique can not increase the robustness because the audio timbre is changed with the sum of pulse amplitude (Oh et al., 2001).

Oh et al. (2001) proposed an echo kernel comprising multiple echoes of both positive and negative pulses with different offsets (closely located) in the kernel, of

Figure 6. Encoding process

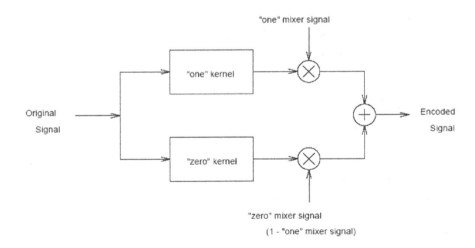

which the frequency response is plain in lower bands and has large ripples in high frequency. Even though they are perceptually less important for most of music, these large ripples can be audible as disagreeable noise for some music sometimes.

Huang et al. (2002) further improved the algorithm in (Oh et al., 2001) by introducing frequency masking to adjust the decays of echo kernels. Those kernels are designed based on the masking threshold so that they remain inaudible after the embedding process. Experiments showed the proposed methods to be more robust to cropping, noise addition and re-sampling than other operations such as filtering and MPEG coding / decoding. This algorithm needs more computation power in calculating the threshold mask and makes it unsuitable for some real time applications.

In order to make echo coding more secure and robust, Ko et al (2002) proposed the time-spread echo method for audio watermarking using PN sequences. In his method, the echo is spread by a pseudorandom number (PN) sequence and then encoded with the original signal. During the decoding process, it is hard to detect the embedded information with only autocepstrum, the general decoding method. The spread kernel is first separated from the watermarked signal by homomorphic processing with cepstral analysis. Then the secret key (PN sequence) used in the encoding process is applied to despread the time-spread echo hidden in the cepstrum. The length of PN sequences and the gain should be long and small to make it robust and imperceptible.

Since there is always a tradeoff between inaudibility and robustness, improving the inaudibility while keeping high robustness is future work.

Echo kernel design seems to be the key point in echo hiding schemes. By introducing multiple echoes, we can reduce the amplitude of each echoes and thus reducing annoying noise. Negative echo is a good idea to reduce the whole added energy to the original signal while keeping the same detection rate. Perceptual analysis in the frequency domain could also be implemented to improve inaudibility. Spreading echo with PN sequence could make echo hiding more robust against malicious detection. A combination of all of above may worth a shot.

4.5 PHASE CODING

Although the human auditory system is extremely more sensitive compared to the human visual system, it is less sensitive to the phase component of the audio. Therefore, we do have some chance to embed watermarks in the phase domain.

The usual procedure for phase coding is as follows (Bender et al., 1996):

a.   Read the input sound (part of the cover work) and break it into N short segments.

b.   Apply DFT to each of the N segments and store the phase and magnitude of each segment

c.   Calculate and store the difference of the neighboring segment.

d.   Let the phase vector of the first signal segment to be $\pi/2$ if the encoded bit is 0 or $-\pi/2$ if the encoded bit is 1

e.   The resulting phase vector should be the addition of the phase vector of the preceding one and the according phase difference we stored in step b.

f.   Use the phase vector from step e and the magnitude from step b and apply inverse DFT to construct the stego-signal.

After the embedding process, the absolute phase in the stego-signal is different than in the original signal, however, the relative phase difference is reserved in the stego-signal which the human ear is most sensitive to. By keeping the relative phase difference untouched, it is possible to make the watermark inaudible.

In the decoding side, some synchronization has to be made before the actual decoding. The length of each segment, the DFT points and the data interval must be known to the decoder. The decoder can use that information to calculate the DFT and to detect the phase vector of the fist signal segment which resembles the encoded message.

Although phase coding is one of the most effective coding methods in terms of the signal-to-perceived noise ratio and capable of embedding inaudible watermark, it has its own disadvantages.

The first one is the distortion introduced to stego-signal caused by the change in the relationship between each frequency component known as phase dispersion. There is a tradeoff between the phase dispersion and audible distortion. The more phase dispersion introduced, the more the insertion data rate we could achieve and the more likely the audible distortion could be produced.

Another distortion is due to the rate of change of the phase modifier. By changing the phase slowly enough, the distortion could be reduced greatly and thus making the watermark inaudible.

Despite all the problems described above, phase coding still plays an important role in digital watermarking due to its potential high capacity and its easy implementation. Inaudible watermarks have been successfully embedded into audio signal by lots of researchers in the past several years.

He et al. (2004) proposed a new phase coding algorithm and the functional representation of the watermarking system is shown in Figure 7. The encoder accepts digital audio and it determines the amount of information that may be inserted in the stereo signal by computing the short-time phase relationship between the two channels. Binary data provided by the auxiliary channel is imperceptibly encoded

Figure 7. Diagram of the proposed phase watermarking coding system

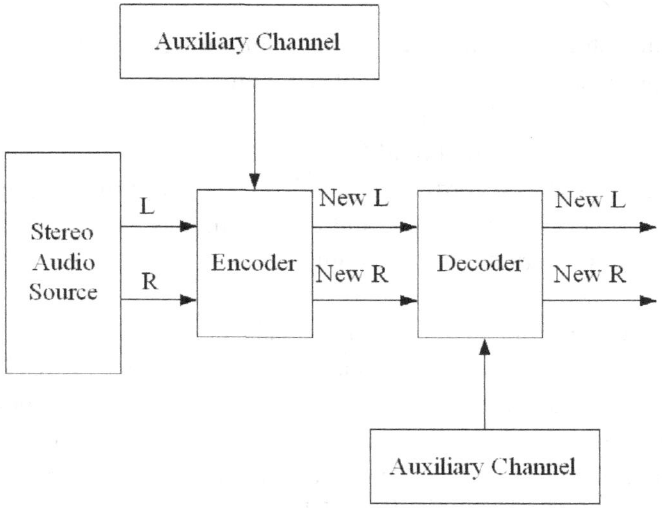

into the phase spectrum of the host audio. The watermarked auxiliary channel is reconstructed at the decoder after the watermark is detected and extracted.

4.6 FRAGILE WATERMARKING

Most of the watermarking schemes require the watermark to survive various attacks, fragile watermarking, on the opposite, ensures the watermark to disappear even under the slightest modification to the original host work, thus, it is commonly used for tamper detection.

Fragile watermarking was first developed for image and video content authentication as assist in maintain and verifying the integrity of its associated cover work. Although there are many other ways to serve the content authentication purpose (for example, appending cryptographic signature to the cover work), fragile watermarking has its own advantages. First of all, since the watermark is embedded into the cover work, there is no need to store the assistant data (cryptographic signature, for instance). Secondly, since the watermark will undergoes the same modification of the cover work, by analyzing the remaining tampered watermark, it might even be possible to find out what, when and where changes have been made to the original cover work. (Cox et al., 2002).

A simple fragile watermarking method involves the LSB replacement where a predefined bit sequence is used to replace the least significant bit of the cover work.

Since any transform or most signal processing applied on the cover work will alter the least significant bit of the audio sample, detection of exactly the same predefined bit sequence implies the work has not been modified with those processes.

This method, although simple, does not guaranty no changes at all have been made to the cover work. Some malicious and sophisticated attacks might make modifications to the cover work while keeping all the LSBs untouched. Researchers have developed more advanced fragile watermarking schemes for better content authentication purpose.

In (Huang, 2009), the author proposed a complex cepstrum domain fragile audio watermarking algorithm based on quantization. Quantization step was determined by the signal to noise ratio (SNR). By analyzing how the changes of the complex ceptrum coefficients is reflected to the time domain signal, the author embedded a fragile watermark to the cover work in complex ceptrum domain. Experiment results show the watermark is fragile to common signal process and cropping attacks making it applicable to signal integrity authentication.

In (Cvejic et al., 2003-a), the authors presented a novel algorithm to embed both robust and fragile watermarks into digital audio signal. The robust watermark is utilized with frequency hopping spread spectrum techniques and the fragile watermark is introduced with LSB modulation, both in discrete wavelet domain. Embedding of the fragile watermark goes as follows:

1. The signal is first segmented into frames of 512 samples long in time domain
2. Each frame is transformed into wavelet domain by five consecutive steps of discrete wavelet decomposing with the simplest quadrature mirror filter (QMF), i.e. Haar filter. This produces 512 wavelet coefficients in 32 subband.
3. All 512 wavelet coefficients are then normalized using the maximum value inside each subband and converted to binary arrays.
4. A fixed number of the LSBs are replaced by the fragile watermark bits.
5. The watermarked work is then transformed back to time domain.

Detection of the fragile watermark is the reverse order of embedding process.

During the evaluation of the fragile watermarking algorithm, the watermarked cover work samples were replaced by random samples. Experimental results showed that the detection system can find out with very high confidence, whether the cover work has been tampered, thus making the algorithm suitable for the digital audio content integrity and authentication application. Furthermore, after locating the incorrect fragile watermark bits, the system can localize the modified content with the spatial information of the wavelet coefficients.

4.7 SPREAD SPECTRUM CODING

The most important and widely used watermarking technology is spread spectrum coding, which will be illustrated in great detail in the next several chapters.

REFERENCES

Bender, W., Gruhl, D., Morimoto, N., & Lu, A. (1996). Techniques for data hiding. *IBM Systems Journal, 35*(3/4), 313–336. doi:10.1147/sj.353.0313

Cox, I. J., Miller, M. L., & Bloom, J. A. (2002). *Digital watermarking.* San Francisco, CA: Academic Press.

Cvejic, N., & Seppänen, T. (2003a). Robust audio watermarking in wavelet domain using frequendy hopping and patchwork method. In *Proceedings of the 3rd International Symposium on Image and Signal Processing and Analysis (ISISPA)* (pp. 251-255).

Gruhl, D., Lu, L., & Bender, W. (1996). Echo hiding. In *Proceedings of the Information Hiding Workshop* (pp.295-315). University of Cambridge, UK.

He, X., Iliev, A., & Scordilis, M. M. (2004). A novel high capacity digital audio watermarking system. In *Proceedings of the IEEE International Conference on Acoustics, Speech and Signal Processing (ICASSP)* (pp. 393-396).

Huang, D. Y., & Yeo, T. Y. (2002). Robust and inaudible multi-echo audio watermarking. In *Proceedings of the IEEE Pacific Rim Conference on Multimedia* (pp.615-622). Taiwan, China.

Huang, X. H. (2009). A complex cepstrum fragile audio watermarking algorithm based on quantization. In *Proceedings of the 3rd International Conference on Genetic and Evolutionary Computing* (pp. 231-234). Guilin, China.

Kim, H. J. (2003). Audio watermarking techniques. In *Proceedings of the Pacific Rim Workshop on Digital Steganography.* Kitakyushu, Japan.

Ko, B. S., Nishimura, R., & Suzuki, Y. (2002). Time-spread echo method for digital audio watermarking using PN sequences. In *Proceedings of the IEEE International Conference on Acoustics, Speech and Signal Processing (ICASSP)* (2, pp. 2001-2004). Orlando, FL.

Oh, H. O., Seok, J. W., Hong, J. W., & Youn, D. H. (2001). New echo embedding technique for robust and imperceptible audio watermarking. In *Proceedings of the IEEE International Conference on Acoustics, Speech and Signal Processing (ICASSP)* (3. pp. 1341-1344). Salt Lake City, UT.

Xu, C., Wu, J., Sun, Q., & Xin, K. (1999). Applications of digital watermarking technology in audio signals. *Journal of the Audio Engineering Society. Audio Engineering Society, 47*(10), 805–812.

Chapter 5
Principles of Spread Spectrum

Since spread spectrum is the most popular technology used in digital watermarking, the next three chapters will focus exclusively on this technology. This chapter will illustrate the principles of spread spectrum.

5.1 THEORY OF SPREAD SPECTRUM TECHNOLOGY IN COMMUNICATION

There are two types of spread spectrum technologies: direct sequence spread spectrum (DSSS) and frequency hopping spread spectrum (FHSS). This section shows the basic principles of these methods as well as a comparison between them.

5.1.1 Direct Sequence Spread Spectrum

DSSS is the technology that employs a pseudo random noise code (PN sequence), which is independent of the signal to be transmitted, and it uses it to modulate or

DOI: 10.4018/978-1-61520-925-5.ch005

Principles of Spread Spectrum

Figure 1. The spread spectrum process in the time domain (Meel, 1999)

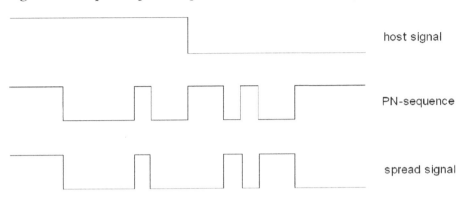

host signal

PN-sequence

spread signal

spread the narrow band signal into a signal with much wider bandwidth. Figure 1 and Figure 2 illustrate this process in the time and frequency domains. At the receiver side, the same PN sequence is used to de-spread the wideband signal back to the original narrowband signal (Meel, 1999).

Power density is the distribution of power over frequency. Although the spread signal has the same amount of energy and carries the same information as the narrow band signal, it has much lower power density due to its much wider bandwidth. This makes it more difficult to detect the existence of the spread spectrum signal. Processing gain is the power density ratio between narrowband signal and spread spectrum signal, which in this case is usually higher than 10 (Chipcenter, 2006).

On the other hand, if the spread signal is contaminated by narrow band jam during transmission the energy of the jam signal will spread over a much wider bandwidth when de-spread, resulting a relatively high signal to noise ratio (SNR) at the receiver which leads to easy detection of the de-spread signal as illustrated in Figure 3. This is the reason for the high robustness of the spread signal against a narrow band jammer.

Figure 2. The spread spectrum process in the frequency domain (Chipcenter, 2006)

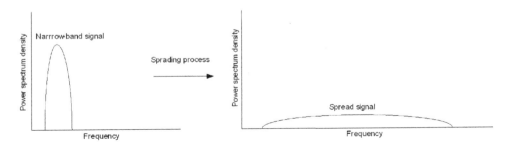

Figure 3. De-spread signal and jammer (Chipcenter, 2006)

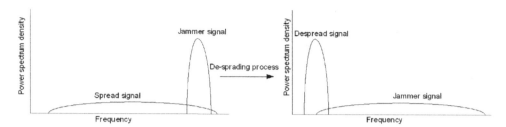

5.1.2 Frequency Hopping Spread Spectrum

Another spread spectrum technology is FHSS which does not spread the narrow band signal into a wideband signal. Instead the frequency of the carrier hops from channel to channel at different times, as shown in Figure 4, and thus it may avoid a jammer operating at some frequency. Since in FHSS the signal does not get spread, there is no processing gain. In order to achieve the same signal-to-noise ratio (SNR) the FHSS system has to output more power than DSSS system.

Since the carrier signal changes frequency from time to time, the sender and the receiver have to be tuned both in time and frequency, which makes synchronization a critical issue. Once it hops, it is very difficult, if not impossible for the receiver to resynchronize in case synchronization is lost. Before the receiver can be synchronized with the sender it has to spend more time to search the signal and to lock on it in time and frequency. This time interval is called lock-in time. FHSS systems need much longer lock-in time than DSSS systems, which only have to synchronize with the timing of the PN sequence.

Figure 4. FHSS illustration (Meel, 1999)

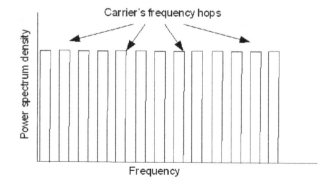

Table 1. Comparison between DSSS and FHSS

	DSSS	**FHSS**
Robustness	High	High
Payload	Low	High
Needs parking frequency	No	Yes
Frequency hops	No	Yes
Synchronization	Easy	Hard
Re-synchronization	Not difficult	Very difficult
Processing gain	High	None
SNR after dispreading	High	Low
Lock-in time	Fast	Slow

In order to make the initial synchronization successful, the hopper needs to park at a fixed frequency before hopping, such frequency is called parking frequency. If unfortunately, the jammer is also located in that frequency the hopper will not be able to hop at all. (Meel, 1999; Chipcenter, 2006).

Despite those disadvantages, the FHSS system can usually carry more data than the DSSS system because the signal is narrowband. It is also harder for opponents to attack the FHSS system than the DSSS system because now the opponent has to track both time and frequency slots to achieve synchronization. A comparison between DSSS and FHSS is shown in Table 1.

5.2 SPREAD SPECTRUM FOR AUDIO WATERMARKING

In this section, spread spectrum technology as it applies to audio watermarking is presented. Substantial work has been carried out in this area and is presented in several key publications (Cox et al, 1997 and 2002; Cvejic, 2004; Gruhl et al., 1996; Bender et al., 1996; Meel, 1999).

Several spread spectrum-based watermarking systems have been proposed since middle 90's when Cox first introduced spread spectrum into watermarking (Cox et al., 1997). A typical frame-based spread spectrum audio watermarking system is illustrated in Figure 5 (encoder) and Figure 6 (decoder). 'F' denotes transform functions (Fourier, DCT, wavelet transform, etc.) and 'IF' is the appropriate inverse transform function.

Figure 5. Typical spread spectrum audio watermarking system; the encoder

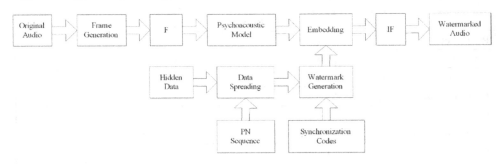

The encoder operates as follows:

a. The input original audio is segmented into overlapped frames of N samples long.
b. If the watermark is to be embedded in the transform domain then each frame is converted into that domain (e.g., frequency, sub band/wavelet or cepstral domain.)
c. A psychoacoustic model is applied to determine the masking thresholds for each frame in order to render the inserted data inaudible.
d. The data are spread by a pseudo random sequence (PN sequence).
e. Synchronization codes are attached to the spread data thus producing the final watermarks to be embedded.
f. Watermark embedding into the original audio is conditional on the masking thresholds constraints.
g. If the watermark is embedded in the transform domain then inverse transform is applied on the watermarked frame to convert the watermarked audio back to the time domain.

Figure 6. Typical spread spectrum audio watermarking system; the decoder

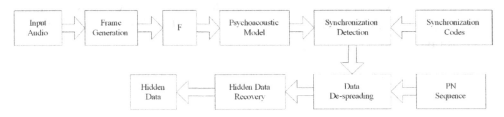

Figure 7. Traditional spread spectrum core (Cvejic, 2004)

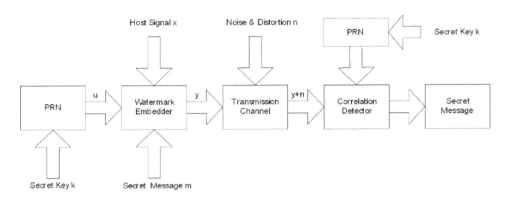

The system decoder works in a reverse manner as in Figure 6 and its operations are:

a. The incoming audio is first segmented into overlapped frames.
b. The frame is converted into transform domain if necessary.
c. The same psychoacoustic model is applied on the data to determine the masking thresholds.
d. Synchronization is performed by searching for the synchronization codes.
e. The appropriate data are then de-spread in order to detect and recover any hidden data.

5.3 ANALYSIS OF TRADITIONAL SS WATERMARKING SYSTEMS

The core part of traditional spread spectrum watermarking is illustrated in Figure 7 where k is the secret key used by a binary pseudo random number generator (PNG) to produce a pseudo random sequence (PN sequence) u with zero mean, and whose elements are either $+\sigma_u$ or $-\sigma_u$. The sequence is then multiplied by the secret message bit m, which is either '1' or '-1', and added to the signal. The watermarked signal s is denoted as:

$$y = x + mu \qquad (5.1)$$

Suppose the watermark bit rate is $1/N$ bits/sample, which means N transformed or time domain samples of the original signal (host signal) are needed to embed one bit of information.

The distortion D caused by embedding is denoted as

$$D = || y - x || = || mu || = || u || = \sigma_u^2 \tag{5.2}$$

where $|| ||$ is the norm defined as $|| x || = \sqrt{< x, x >}$
and $<>$ is the inner product calculated as

$$< x, u > = \sum_{i=0}^{N-1} x_i u_i \tag{5.3}$$

and N is the vector length of x and u.

Noise n is considered to be additive in the channel and the received signal in the decoding side is modeled as

$$\hat{y} = y + n \tag{5.4}$$

Normalized correlation is performed between the received signal and the PN sequence u to extract the watermark as follows

$$r = \frac{< \hat{y}, u >}{< u, u >} = \frac{< mu + x + n, u >}{\sigma_u^2} = m + x_u + n_u \tag{5.5}$$

where $x_u = \dfrac{< x, u >}{\sigma_u^2}$ and $n_u = \dfrac{< n, u >}{\sigma_u^2}$ (5.6)

Usually x and n are considered Gaussian sequences as $x \sim N(0, \sigma_x^2)$ and $n \sim N(0, \sigma_n^2)$.

Un-correlation between x and u is assumed when the lengths of both vectors are large enough and it leads to $x_u \approx 0$. The same assumption applies to n and u which leads to $n_u \approx 0$.

Therefore the recovered watermark is denoted as

$$\hat{m} = sign(r) \tag{5.7}$$

Figure 8. Typical result of the linear correlation

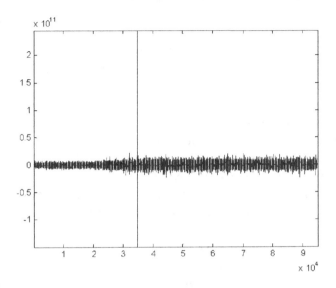

Normalized correlation r is considered also a Gaussian process as

$$r \sim N(m_r, \sigma_r^2) \text{ and } m_r = E(r) = m\sigma_r^2 = \frac{\sigma_x^2 + \sigma_n^2}{N\sigma_u^2} \tag{5.8}$$

The equal error extraction probability p is given by

$$p = \Pr\{\hat{m} < 0 \mid m = 1\} =$$
$$\Pr\{\hat{m} > 0 \mid m = -1\} = \tag{5.9}$$
$$\frac{1}{2}erfc\left(\frac{m_r}{\sigma_r\sqrt{2}}\right) = \frac{1}{2}erfc\left(\sqrt{\frac{N\sigma_u^2}{2(\sigma_x^2 + \sigma_n^2)}}\right)$$

where *erfc()* is the complementary error function.

Figure 8 shows the typical result of the linear correlation and we can easily see the spike where watermark is embedded.

5.4 PROBLEMS OF TRADITIONAL SS WATERMARKING SYSTEMS

Although direct SS has the advantages including no original cover work needed during detection and relatively high robustness which make it so popular, it does have its own disadvantages including:

a. The marked signal and the watermark (WM) or PN sequence have to be perfectly synchronized during the detection process.
b. WM length has to be long enough to achieve acceptable error probability, thus increasing detection complexity and delay
c. As explained in (Kirovski et al., 2003) and (Malyar et al. 2003), in traditional SS the signal itself is seen as a source of interference which may degrade the audio quality.
d. Maximum length sequence (M-sequence) is usually used as pseudo-random sequence (PN sequence) which has two disadvantages. One is that length of chip rate is strictly limited to as given by (2^M-1). For example, 1023 and 2047 are the usually lengths used. Second, the number of different M-sequence is also limited once the size M is determined, thus making it insecure in terms of cryptography.
e. When dealing with compressed watermarked audio signal, most systems have to introduce a whole decompression to perform the detection process which adds to a time delay.

REFERENCES

Bender, W., Gruhl, D., Morimoto, N., & Lu, A. (1996). Techniques for data hiding. *IBM Systems Journal*, *35*(3/4), 313–336. doi:10.1147/sj.353.0313

Chipcenter. (2006). Tutorial on spread spectrum. Retrieved from http://archive. chipcenter.com/ knowledge_centers/digital/ features/showArticle.jhtml? articleID=9901240

Cox, I. J., Kilian, J., Leighton, T., & Shamoon, T. (1997). Secure spread spectrum watermarking for multimedia. *IEEE Transactions on Image Processing*, *6*(12), 1673–1687. doi:10.1109/83.650120

Cox, I. J., Miller, M. L., & Bloom, J. A. (2002). *Digital watermarking*. San Francisco, CA: Academic Press.

Cvejic, N. (2004). *Algorithms for audio watermarking and steganography*, (Unpublished doctoral dissertation), University of Oulu, Oulu, Finland. Retrieved from http://herkules.oulu.fi/ isbn9514273842/ isbn9514273842.pdf

Gruhl, D., Lu, L., & Bender, W. (1996). Echo hiding. In *Proceedings of the Information Hiding Workshop* (pp.295-315). University of Cambridge, UK.

Kirovski, D., & Malvar, H. S. (2003). Spread-spectrum watermarking of audio signals. *IEEE Transactions on Signal Processing, 51*(4), 1020–1033. doi:10.1109/TSP.2003.809384

Malvar, H. S., & Florencio, D. A. (2003). Improved spread spectrum: a new modulation technique for robust audio watermarking. *IEEE Transactions on Signal Processing, 51*(4), 898–905. doi:10.1109/TSP.2003.809385

Meel Ir. J. (1999). Spread spectrum (SS) introduction, *Denyer Institute Report*. Retrieved from http://www.sss-mag.com /pdf/Ss_jme_denayer _intro_print.pdf

Chapter 6
Survey of Spread Spectrum Based Audio Watermarking Schemes

This chapter presents the survey of spread spectrum based audio watermarking schemes in the literature.

6.1 BASIC DIRECT SEQUENCE SPREAD SPECTRUM

Cox et al. (1997) proposed a secure robust watermarking approach for multimedia based on spread spectrum technology. Although their system was originally proposed for watermarking images the basic idea also applies to audio watermarking.

The watermarking procedure proceeds as follows:

From host signal, a sequence of values $x=\{x_i\}$ is extracted, which is used for inserting secret message $m=\{m_i\}$. The watermarked sequence is denoted as $w' = \{w'_i\}$ and inserted back into the place of x to obtain a watermarked signal y. During

DOI: 10.4018/978-1-61520-925-5.ch006

transmission, possible distortion or attacks may affect y and the received signal is now denoted as $\hat{y}$, which may not be identical to y. Assume the host signal is available at the decoder side, a probably altered watermarked sequence $w^* = \{w_i^*\}$ is first extracted from the received signal $\hat{y}$. A possibly corrupted message m^* is extracted from w^* and compared to m for statistical significance. (Cox et al., 1997).

During watermark embedding, a scaling parameter α which controls the watermark strength is specified and used in the watermark embedding equation. Three embedding formulae used are

$$y = x + \alpha w \tag{6.1}$$

$$y = x(1 + \alpha w) \tag{6.2}$$

$$y = x(e^{\alpha w}) \tag{6.3}$$

Equation (6.2) is used in (Cox, 1997) with α = 0.1.

The similarity between the extracted watermark and the embedded watermark is measured by

$$sim(m, m^*) = \frac{m.m^*}{\sqrt{m^*.m^*}} \tag{6.4}$$

Large values of $sim(m, m^*)$ are important and typically if $sim(m, m^*) > 6$, then a watermark is detected in the received signal.

6.2 TIME DOMAIN SPREAD SPECTRUM WATERMARKING SCHEME

Cvejic et al. (2004) proposed an alternative audio spread spectrum watermarking scheme in the time domain. The embedding part is illustrated in Figure 1.

Time domain masking properties of the HAS are used to maximize the amplitude of the watermark to be embedded, which increases robustness during detection, while still keeping the watermark imperceptible and maintaining high perceptual audio quality.

A frequency analysis block counts the signal zero-crossing-rate (ZCR) in the basic block interval and derives the high frequency spectral information. The power of the embedded watermark is proportional to the amount and strength of high frequency

Figure 1. Spread spectrum watermarking in the time domain (Cvejic, 2004)

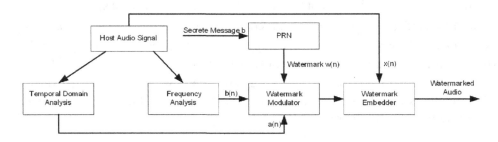

components in the spectrum. The purpose of this frequency domain analysis is to further increase the power of the watermark without jeopardizing the perceptual quality of the audio signal.

Let $a(n)$ and $b(n)$ be the coefficients obtained from temporal and frequency analysis blocks respectively, $x(n)$ be the original audio and $w(n)$ be the spread watermark in the time domain. Then the watermarked audio $y(n)$ is denoted by

$$y(n) = x(n) + a(n)b(n)w(n) \qquad (6.5)$$

Figure 2 provides a functional diagram of the watermark detection algorithm, which is based on a cross-correlation calculation. The novelty of this detection lies in the mean-removed cross-correlation between the watermarked audio signal and the equalized m-sequence. The watermarked audio is first processed by a high pass equalization filter, which filters out the strong low pass components increases the correlation value and enhances the detection result.

An adaptive filter, instead of a fixed coefficient one, is employed as the equalization filter to better accommodate the input audio. The output from the correlation calculation block is sampled by the detection and sampling block. The result is

Figure 2. Watermarking detection algorithm proposed in (Cvejic, 2004)

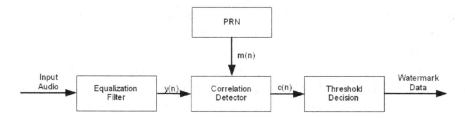

forwarded to the threshold detection block, which uses the majority rule to decide the value of the embedded watermark bit.

6.3 SPREAD SPECTRUM WATERMARKING WITH PSYCHOACOUSTIC MODEL AND 2-D INTERLEAVING ARRAY

Garcia (1999) introduced a digital audio watermarking that uses a psychoacoustic model and spread spectrum theory. In this method, a psychoacoustic model similar to moving picture expert group (MPEG) I Layer 1 is used to derive the masking thresholds from the original host audio signal. The watermark is generated with direct sequence spread spectrum and transformed into the frequency domain. Noise shaping is applied on the watermark to ensure transparent embedding.

The innovation part of this method lies in the two-dimension matrix used to enhance the watermark robustness. Here the watermark is first repeated for M times (Kirovski et al., 2003) and then interleaved by a *2-D* array. The purpose of the *2-D* array interleaving is to enhance the robustness against additive noise, especially pulse-like noise.

Suppose the data to be embedded comprise N samples denoted by $\{m_i\}$ consisting of '1's and '-1's ('0's in the watermark are transformed into '-1' to enhance the robustness). First every sample in $\{m_i\}$ is locally repeated M times resulting in the sequence: $\{m_1 m_1 m_1 ... m_2 m_2 m_2 ... m_N m_N ... m_N\}$.

The new data sequence is interleaved by a *2-D* array with the size $N*M$ (N rows by M columns), the above sequence is used to form an array row-by-row and read out column by column to form a new data sequence as: $\{m_1 m_2 ... m_N m_1 m_2 ... m_N ... m_1 m_2 ... m_N\}$.

Suppose more than $M/2$ samples of the same symbol in the un-interleaved watermark are corrupted by noise during transmission or attack. Then the symbol cannot be recovered at the decoder end. However, if the watermark is interleaved before embedding, there will be a better chance to recover it later.

As an illustrative example, suppose the data *{m}* to be embed is a '*1001*', and since '0's are transformed into '-1's, the watermark data *{w}* become '*1 -1 -1 1*'. Then each symbol repeats M times (let $M = 5$) and the sequence now becomes '*1 1 1 1 1 -1 -1 -1 -1 -1 -1 -1 -1 -1 -1 1 1 1 1 1*'. The repeated data is written into a 5*4 *2-D* array in rows as shown in Table 1.

The data is now read out column-by-column into before embedding resulting in a new sequence: '*1 -1 -1 1 1 -1 -1 1 1 -1 -1 1 1 -1 -1 1 1 -1 -1 1*'.

Suppose that during transmission, the first 8 symbols become corrupted, and the decoder receives instead the sequence '*x x x x x x x x 1 1 -1 -1 1 1 -1 -1 1 1 -1 -1*

Table 1. Data interleaving example

1	1	1	1	1
-1	-1	-1	-1	-1
-1	-1	-1	-1	-1
1	1	1	1	1

Table 2. Data de-interleaving example

X	X	1	1	1
X	X	-1	-1	-1
X	X	-1	-1	-1
X	X	1	1	1

1' where 'x' denotes unknown symbol ('1' or '-1'). De-interleaving is performed on the received sequence by writing it into the same *2-D* array by column resulting in the matrix of Table 2.

The data in the de-interleaving array are read out by row and we have '*x x 1 1 1 x x -1 -1 -1 x x -1 -1 -1 x x 1 1 1*'.

The decision rule for the k-th symbol of the recovered watermark is

$$
w_k = \begin{cases} 1 & if \ r_k > 0 \\ -1 & if \ r_k \leq 0 \end{cases} \tag{6.6}
$$

where

$$
r_k = \sum_{i=(k-1)*M+1}^{k*M} m_i \tag{6.7}
$$

M is the repetition number (*M = 5* in this example), m_i is the i-th symbol in the above sequence.

According to the decision rule:

$$
r_1 = r_4 = x + x + 1 + 1 + 1 = 3 + 2 * x > 0
$$

$$
r_2 = r_3 = x + x - 1 - 1 - 1 = -3 + 2 * x < 0
$$

so $w_1=w_4=1$ and $w_2=w_3=-1$ and the recovered watermark is: '1 -1 -1 1', which is identical to the embedded.

By interleaving the embedded watermark the possible additive noise is averaged by factor equal to the number of rows in the *2-D* array. On the other hand, if no interleave is involved during the embedding process the sequence that the decoder received will be '*x x x x x x x x -1 -1 -1 -1 -1 -1 -1 1 1 1 1 1*'. We can easily see that the decoder can only recover the last two symbols correctly while the first two symbols are lost.

6.4 AN IMPROVED SPREAD SPECTRUM METHOD

An improved spread spectrum (ISS) method, which uses a new modulation technique for increased watermark robustness was proposed by Malvar and Florencio (2003). In spread spectrum approaches, the host signal is considered as interference to the embedded watermark and affects the detection in the negative way. In ISS, the knowledge of the projection of the host signal (x_u in Equation 6.8) on the watermark is used to modulate the energy of the watermark, thus improving the detection performance. The new embedding rule is defined as:

$$y = x + \mu(x_u, b)u \tag{6.8}$$

where

$$x_u = \frac{<x, u>}{\sigma_u^2} \tag{6.9}$$

The traditional SS is a special case of ISS where the function μ is independent of x_u. A simple linear function is used in this method and the embedding function now becomes

$$y = x + (\alpha b - \lambda x_u)u \tag{6.10}$$

The parameter α controls the distortion level caused by watermark embedding and λ controls the removal of host signal distortion. it can be noted that traditional spread spectrum is a special case of ISS with $\alpha=1$ and $\lambda=0$.

The normalized correlation now becomes

$$r = \frac{<y, u>}{|| u ||} = \alpha b + (1 - \lambda)x_u + x_n \qquad (6.11)$$

As we can see from above equation, the more λ approaches 1 the less the influence of the host signal distortion on the watermark detection. Parameter α is chosen in a way that the distortion in the ISS is equal to the distortion in the SS.

The expected distortion in ISS is

$$E[D] = E[|| y - x ||] =$$
$$E[| \alpha b - \lambda x_u |^2 \sigma_u^2] = (\alpha^2 + \frac{\lambda^2 \sigma_x^2}{N\sigma_u^2})\sigma_u^2 \qquad (6.12)$$

Comparing this to Equation (6.10) we have

$$\alpha = \sqrt{\frac{N\sigma_u^2 - \lambda^2\sigma_x^2}{N\sigma_u^2}} \qquad (6.13)$$

The mean and variance of r are given by

$$m_r = \alpha b \qquad (6.14)$$

and

$$\sigma_r^2 = \frac{\sigma_n^2 + (1 - \lambda)^2\sigma_x^2}{N\sigma_u^2} \qquad (6.15)$$

The error probability of ISS is calculated as

$$p = \Pr\{\hat{m} < 0 \mid m = 1\} =$$

$$\Pr\{\hat{m} > 0 \mid m = -1\} = \frac{1}{2} erfc\left(\frac{m_r}{\sigma_r \sqrt{2}}\right) = \tag{6.16}$$

$$\frac{1}{2} erfc\left(\sqrt{\frac{N\sigma_u^2 - \lambda^2 \sigma_x^2}{2(\sigma_n^2 + (1-\lambda)^2 \sigma_x^2)}}\right) = \frac{1}{2} erfc\left(\frac{1}{\sqrt{2}}\sqrt{\frac{\frac{N\sigma_u^2}{\sigma_x^2} - \lambda^2}{\frac{\sigma_u^2}{\sigma_x^2} + (1-\lambda)^2)}}\right)$$

The host signal is considered noise for watermark detection. The resulting watermark-to-noise ratio (WNR) is $\frac{\sigma_u^2}{\sigma_x^2}$.

By selecting an appropriate λ, the ISS can lead to an error rate several orders lower than traditional SS method. The optimal parameter of λ is given by

$$\lambda_{opt} =$$

$$\frac{1}{2}\left((1 + \frac{\sigma_n^2}{\sigma_x^2} + \frac{N\sigma_u^2}{\sigma_x^2}) - \sqrt{(1 + \frac{\sigma_n^2}{\sigma_x^2} + \frac{N\sigma_u^2}{\sigma_x^2})^2 - 4\frac{N\sigma_u^2}{\sigma_x^2}}\right) \tag{6.17}$$

6.5 NOVEL SPREAD SPECTRUM APPROACH

Kirovski et al. (2001, 2002 and 2003) gradually and systematically developed a novel spread spectrum approach for audio signals. The key features of this method include:

a.   Block repetition coding for prevention against de-synchronization attacks
b.   Psycho-acoustic frequency masking (PAFM)
c.   A modified covariance test to compensate the imbalance in the number of positive and negative watermark chips in the audible part of the frequency spectrum
d.   Cepstral filtering and chess watermarks are used to reduce the variance of the correlation test, thus improving reliability of watermark detection.
e.   A special procedure used to identify the audibility of spread spectrum watermarks

f.   A technique which enables reliable covert communication over public audio channel

g.   A secure spread spectrum watermark that survives watermark estimation attacks

Feature *e* is particularly worth noting and it will further be expanded upon in a later section. Detailed illustration of other features can be found in (Kirovski and Attias, 2002).

In order to embed spread spectrum WM imperceptibly, blocks with dynamic content are detected prior to watermark embedding. These blocks have some quiet parts and other parts rich in audio energy. Embedding watermarks into the quite parts will result in audible distortion even is the amplitude of watermarks is low.

The procedure of detecting the problematic audio data blocks is as follows:

a.   The signal is divided into blocks of K samples

b.   Each block is further partitioned into P interleaved subintervals

c.   The interval energy level is computed as $E(i) = \sum_{j=1+K(i-1)/(2P)}^{iK/P} y_j, i = 1...P$ for each of the P subintervals of the tested signal y in the time domain

d.   If $\min_{1 \leq j \leq P}(E(j) / \sum_{i=1}^{P} E(i)) \leq x_0$, then the watermark is audible in this block where x_0 is an experimentally obtained threshold

Those problematic blocks are not used for watermark embedding or detection.

6.6 ENHANCED SPREAD SPECTRUM WATERMARKING FOR AAC AUDIO

While the above spread spectrum watermarking methods can successfully embed watermarks into uncompressed audio none of them can deal effectively with audio in compressed domains. Cheng et al. (2002) proposed enhanced spread spectrum watermarking for compressed audio in MPEG-2 AAC (Advanced Audio Coding) format.

The novelty of their methods lies in two contributions:

a.   An enhanced spread spectrum technique, which reduces the variance of the host signal and enhances watermark detection. This contribution will be further analyzed in a later section.

b. Direct embedding of watermarks into the quantization indices instead of the modified discrete cosine transform (MDCT) coefficients, which saves processing time since no de-quantization or re-quantization is necessary. Here a heuristic approach is used to select the indices and estimate the strength that those indices should be scaled to. Three steps are involved for the heuristic approach:

  i. Pick indices located at frequencies where the HAS is more sensitive and therefore they are perceptually important. This enhanced the watermark robustness by preventing frequency truncation attack.

  ii. Indices with zero values are not selected to avoid introducing the audible distortion of embedding watermark into silent areas.

  iii. Quantization step is set to 1 to minimize distortion.

This method is low in both structural and computational complexity because only Huffman encoding and decoding are required to embed and estimate the watermark. The heuristic estimation on the perceptual weighting of the indices, which provides acceptable perceptual quality, is much simpler than incorporating a full psychoacoustic model.

Even though the most popular spread spectrum is DSSS and the key techniques have been presented, frequency hopping spread spectrum (FHSS) can also used for watermarking.

6.7 FREQUENCY HOPPING SPREAD SPECTRUM

Cvejic and Seppänen (2003a) proposed an audio watermarking based on FHSS and so called "attack characterization" to battle against some limitations of spread spectrum based on direct sequence. Based on the observation that if the watermarked signal undergoes fading-like attacks, such as MPEG compressing or LP filtering for instance, the correlation between the host signal and the watermark can result in ineffective detection because those attacks cannot be modeled as additive white Gaussian noise (AWGN), it is claimed that a far more appropriate model is the frequency selective model, which takes into account more precisely the distortion introduced by those fading attacks.

In their method, characterization of the MPEG compression watermarking attack is analyzed first to find out the subset of FFT coefficients that are least distorted by the attack. Frequency hopping spread spectrum (FHSS) is used to select two FFT coefficients from those least vulnerable subsets. The real watermark embedding is performed by the patchwork algorithm. If bit 1 is to be embedded, the magnitude of the lower frequency coefficient is increased by K decibels and the magnitude of

Figure 3. Example of frequency hopping used during watermark embedding (Cvejic and Seppänen, 2003a)

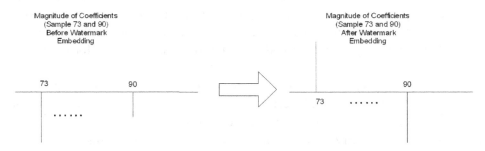

higher frequency coefficient is decreased by the same amount. If bit 0 is to be embedded, the opposite operation is performed. An example of the frequency hopping method used during watermark embedding is illustrated in Figure 3.

By using the frequency hopping method different FFT coefficient pairs are selected to embed watermarks in each block, making the watermark location very tough to guess by opponents.

6.8 LIMITS OF TRADITIONAL SPREAD SPECTRUM METHOD

Although many spread spectrum based audio watermarking systems have been developed by researchers as mentioned above, most of those watermarking systems however, share some common issues due to the limits of the spread spectrum including:

a.   Interference between the embedded watermarks and the host signal;
b.   Synchronizing problem between the watermarking encoder and decoder.

Chapter 7 introduces some improved spread spectrum detecting methods to solve the interference limit. An improved synchronization solution is proposed in Chapter 12.

REFERENCES

Cheng, S., Yu, H., & Xiong, Z. (2002). Enhanced spread spectrum watermarking of MPEG-2 AAC audio. In *Proceedings of the IEEE International Conference on Acoustics, Speech and Signal Processing (ICASSP)* (4, pp. 3728-3731). Orlando, FL.

Cox, I. J., Kilian, J., Leighton, T., & Shamoon, T. (1997). Secure spread spectrum watermarking for multimedia. *IEEE Transactions on Image Processing, 6*(12), 1673–1687. doi:10.1109/83.650120

Cvejic, N. (2004). *Algorithms for audio watermarking and steganography*, (Unpublished doctoral dissertation), University of Oulu, Oulu, Finland. Retrieved from http://herkules.oulu.fi/ isbn9514273842/ isbn9514273842.pdf

Cvejic, N., & Seppänen, T. (2003a). Robust audio watermarking in wavelet domain using frequendy hopping and patchwork method. In *Proceedings of the 3rd International Symposium on Image and Signal Processing and Analysis (ISISPA)* (pp. 251-255).

Garcia, R. A. (1999). Digital watermarking of audio signals using a psychoacoustic model and spread spectrum theory. In *Proceedings of the 107th Convention of Audio Engineering Society (AES)*, New York, NY (Preprint 5073).

Kirovski, D., & Attias, H. (2002). Audio watermark robustness to de-synchronization via beat detection. In *Proceedings of the 5th International Workshop on Information Hiding* (pp. 160-176). Noordwijkerhout, Netherlands.

Kirovski, D., & Malvar, H. S. (2001). Robust spread-spectrum audio watermarking. In *Proceedings of the IEEE International Conference on Acoustics, Speech and Signal Processing (ICASSP)* (3, pp. 1345-1348). Salt Lake City, UT.

Kirovski, D., & Malvar, H. S. (2003). Spread-spectrum watermarking of audio signals. *IEEE Transactions on Signal Processing, 51*(4), 1020–1033. doi:10.1109/TSP.2003.809384

Malvar, H. S., & Florencio, D. A. (2003). Improved spread spectrum: a new modulation technique for robust audio watermarking. *IEEE Transactions on Signal Processing, 51*(4), 898–905. doi:10.1109/TSP.2003.809385

Chapter 7
Techniques for Improved Spread Spectrum Detection

In this chapter, techniques for improved spread spectrum detection are reviewed.

A typical detection method for spread spectrum is the computation of the cross-correlation between the received stego-signal and the actual watermark. If the computed output exceeds a threshold then a watermark is considered to have been detected in the received signal.

7.1 MATCHED FILTER APPROACH

Some watermarking system employs a pseudo random sequence (PN sequence) for synchronization purpose. Matched filter is usually used in such cases to detect the existence of the PN sequence and to precisely locate the starting sample of the PN sequence.

DOI: 10.4018/978-1-61520-925-5.ch007

In the watermarking system, the PN sequence is considered as noise added to the host signal. Since the PN sequence only lasts a very short period of time, it could be treated as transient noise pulses and detected by a filter whose impulse response is matched to the PN sequence. Such is the matched filter whose frequency response is defined as (Vaseghi, 2000):

$$H(f) = K \frac{PN^*(f)}{PSx(f)} \tag{7.1}$$

Where K is a scaling factor, $PN^*(f)$ is the complex conjugate of the spectrum of PN sequence $\{u\}$ and $PSx(f)$ is the power spectrum of the host signal x.

In real world applications, the host signal is very close to a zero mean process with variance σ_x^2 and is uncorrelated to the PN sequence. Then, Equation (7.1) becomes

$$H(f) = \frac{K}{\sigma_x^2} PN^*(f) \tag{7.2}$$

with impulse response

$$h(n) = \frac{K}{\sigma_x^2} u(-n) \tag{7.3}$$

When the received signal contains the PN sequence, it is defined as

$$y(n) = x(n) + \alpha u(n) \tag{7.4}$$

where α is a strength control factor. Then the output of the matched filter is

$$
\begin{aligned}
o(n) &= \frac{K}{\sigma_x^2} u(-n) * (x(j) + \alpha u(j)) \\
&= \frac{K}{\sigma_x^2} u(-n) * x(j) + \frac{\alpha K}{\sigma_x^2} u(-n) * u(j) \\
&= d_{\mu x} + d_{\mu}
\end{aligned}
\tag{7.5}
$$

Figure 1. Typical result of the correlation output

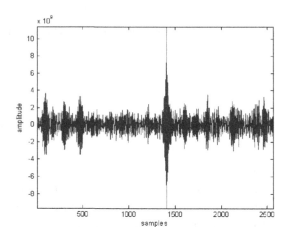

Since the host signal and PN sequence are uncorrelated, $d_{\mu x}$ is expected to be zero. The PN sequence itself is orthogonal to the host signal, and so d_μ will reach its maximum if the sequence is perfectly aligned, otherwise, it will be zero.

Therefore, the detected starting location of the PN sequence in a block will be

$$pn_{loc} = \arg \max_i (o(n)) \tag{7.6}$$

Figure 1 shows a typical output of such matched filter. Note that the peak location marks the beginning of the embedded PN sequence.

The described matched filter detection is optimal for additive white Gaussian noise (Cvejic, 2004). However, the host audio signal is usually far from being white Gaussian noise. Adjacent audio sample are usually highly correlated with large variance, which increases the detection error for spread spectrum. Several techniques have been developed to decrease such correlation.

7.2 SAVITZKY-GOLAY SMOOTHING FILTERS

Cvejic (2004) applied least squares Savitzky-Golay smoothing filters in the time domain to smooth out a wideband noise audio signal. By doing so the variance of the host audio signal is greatly reduced.

Let's recall the equal error extraction probability p as given by

$$p = \Pr\{\hat{m} < 0 \mid m = 1\} = \Pr\{\hat{m} > 0 \mid m =$$

$$-1\} = \frac{1}{2} erfc\left(\frac{m_r}{\sigma_r \sqrt{2}}\right) = \frac{1}{2} erfc\left(\sqrt{\frac{N\sigma_u^2}{2(\sigma_x^2 + \sigma_n^2)}}\right) \tag{7.7}$$

It is clear that a reduced variance σ_x will result in a decreased detection error rate.

Another way to decrease the audio signal variance is so called whitening process, which subtracts a moving average from the frequency spectrum of the received signal right before correlation. This method, although it removes part of the correlation in the audio signal, it also removes part of the watermark as well since the watermarks are spread all over the frequency spectrum.

7.3 CEPSTRUM FILTERING

Kirovski et al. (2001) proposed a cepstrum filtering method to reduce the variance which works as follows:

a. The received signal is a modulated complex lapped transform (MCLT) vector y.
b. Compute the cepstrum of the dB magnitude MCLT vector y by the Discrete Cosine Transform. $Z=DCT(y)$
c. Filter out the first K cepstral coefficients. $z_i=0, i=1 \ldots K$
d. Inverse DCT is applied to z and the output is used by the correlation detector.

The idea behind this method is that large variations in the received signal y can only come from large variations in the host signal x, considering that the watermark magnitude is low. By removing large variations in y, the variance of the host signal x is greatly reduced resulting a better detection performance.

7.4 SPECTRAL ENVELOP FILTERING

Another way to improve the detection is to minimize the effect of the original signal on the correlation. During detection, the host signal is considered as noise which degrades the detection performance due to its strong energy. This effect is much worse in audio watermarking compared to image watermarking since the human auditory system is more sensitive than human visual system. Audible distortion is prevented by keeping the magnitude of the watermark low which however leads to small watermark to signal ratio (SNR) at the detection phase.

In order to blindly remove the effects of host signal for better audio watermark extraction, Jung et al. (2003) proposed a method they called spectral envelop filtering.

This method removes the spectral envelop of the received stego signal and reduces the noise variance of the correlation value at the detector. Since most of the spectral features in the spectral envelope of the watermarked signal come from host signal, filtering the spectral envelope will reduce the effects of the host signal and improve watermark detection. The steps of this method are:

a.   Low pass filter (LPF) the input watermarked signal spectrum X to get the spectral envelop vector Y in dB.

$$Y = LPF(\log(X)) \tag{7.8}$$

b.   Remove Y from $log(X)$
c.   Convert the filtered data into linear scale

$$\hat{X} = e^{(\log(X)-Y)} \tag{7.9}$$

According to their experiments, the spectral envelop filtering method improves the detection performance by 1 to 2 orders.

7.5 THE LINEAR PREDICTION METHOD

Seok et al. (2002) introduced a method base on linear prediction (LP) as a way to remove the correlation in the audio signal. Using LP, the original audio signal $x(n)$ is estimated by the past p audio samples as

$$\hat{x}(n) = a_1 x(n-1) + a_2 x(n-2) + ... + a_p x(n-p) \tag{7.10}$$

where the LP coefficients $a_1, a_2 ... a_p$ are fixed over the audio analysis frame.

If the error between $x(n)$ and its estimation is denoted as $e(n)$ then

$$x(n) = \hat{x}(n) + e(n) \tag{7.11}$$

the watermarked signal *y(n)* becomes

$$y(n) = x(n) + w(n) = \hat{x}(n) + ex(n) + w(n) =$$
$$\sum_{i=1}^{p} a_i x(n-i) + e(n) + w(n) \qquad (7.12)$$

Applying linear prediction to *y(n)* we have

$$y(n) = \hat{y}(n) + e(n) = \sum_{i=1}^{p} a_i y(n-i) + e(n) \qquad (7.13)$$

where $\hat{y}(n) = \sum_{i=1}^{p} a_i y(n-i)$ is the estimation of $y(n)$ and $e(n) = y(n) - \hat{y}(n)$ is the residual signal of *y(n)*, which characterizes both the watermark *w(n)* and the residual signal of *x(n)*.

An example of this method is illustrated in Figure 2 where (a) is the probability density function (pdf) of watermarked audio and (b) is the pdf of its residual signal. It is evident that the watermarked signal has large variance while its residual signal is smoothed out by the LP operation and has a much smaller variance. The residual signal and the PN sequence are used as input to a matched filter. The watermark recovery bit error rate with LP is greatly reduced compared to the non-LP detection.

7.6 DE-SYNCHRONIZATION ATTACKS AND TRADITIONAL SOLUTIONS

While spread spectrum is robust to many attacks including noise addition it remains susceptible to de-synchronization attacks. De-synchronization attacks aim at removing / attacking the synchronization code embedded before the watermark, thus disrupt the synchronization between the watermark encoder and decoder. Without such synchronization information, the watermark decoder does not know the starting location of the embedded watermark, thus failing to recover the original watermark.

It is relatively easy to employ de-synchronization attacks on spread spectrum watermarking system and create catastrophic damages. Traditional solutions to the de-synchronization attacks include exhaustive search; redundant watermark embedding; invariant domain embedding; using synchronization marks; using self-synchronized watermarks; feature points or content synchronization. Those

Figure 2. Example probability density functions of the LP method for one audio frame (Seok et al., 2002)

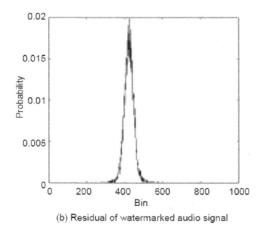

(b) Residual of watermarked audio signal

traditional solutions will be explained in detail in Chapter 12. Moreover, a novel synchronization method will also be presented in that Chapter.

REFERENCES

Cvejic, N. (2004). *Algorithms for audio watermarking and steganography* (Unpublished doctoral dissertation), University of Oulu, Oulu, Finland. Retrieved from http://herkules.oulu.fi /isbn9514273842/ isbn9514273842.pdf

Jung, S., Seok, J., & Hong, J. (2003). An improved detection technique for spread spectrum audio watermarking with a spectral envelope filter. *ETRI*, *25*(1), 52–54. doi:10.4218/etrij.03.0203.0103

Kirovski, D., & Malvar, H. S. (2001). Robust spread-spectrum audio watermarking. In *Proceedings of the IEEE International Conference on Acoustics, Speech and Signal Processing (ICASSP)* (3, pp. 1345-1348). Salt Lake City, UT.

Seok, J., Hong, J., & Kim, J. (2002). A novel audio watermarking algorithm for copyright protection of digital audio. *ETRI Journal*, *24*(3), 181–189. doi:10.4218/ etrij.02.0102.0301

Vaseghi, S. V. (2000). *Advanced digital signal processing and noise reduction*. Hoboken, NJ: John Wiley & Sons, Ltd.

Chapter 8
A Psychoacoustic Model Based on the Discrete Wavelet Packet Transform

The perception of acoustic information by humans is based on the detailed temporal and spectral analysis provided by the auditory processing of the received signal. The incorporation of this process in psychoacoustical computational models has contributed significantly both in the development of highly efficient audio compression schemes as well as in effective audio watermarking methods. In this chapter, we present an approach based on the discrete wavelet packet transform, which closely mimics the multi-resolution properties of the human ear and also includes simultaneous and temporal auditory masking. Experimental results show that the proposed technique offers better masking capabilities and it reduces the signal-to-masking ratio when compared to related approaches, without introducing audible distortion. Those results have implications that are important both for audio compression by permitting further bit rate reduction and for watermarking by providing greater signal space for information hiding.

DOI: 10.4018/978-1-61520-925-5.ch008

8.1 INTRODUCTION

Psychoacoustic modeling has made important contributions in the development of recent high quality audio compression methods (ISO/IEC 11172-3, 1993; Painter and Spanias, 2000; Pan, 1995) and has enabled the introduction of effective audio watermarking techniques (Swanson et al., 1998; Liu, 2004; Cox et al., 2002). In audio analysis and coding, it strives to reduce the signal information rate in lossy signal compression, while maintaining transparent quality. This is achieved by accounting for auditory masking effects, which make possible to keep quantization and processing noises inaudible. In speech and audio watermarking the inclusion of auditory masking has made possible the addition of information that is unrelated to the signal in a manner that keeps it imperceptible and can be effectively recovered during the identification process.

Most psychoacoustic models used in audio compression or watermarking, have so far utilized the short-time Fourier transform (STFT) to construct a time-varying spectral representation of the signal (Painter and Spanias, 2000; Cox, 1997; Bosi and Goldberg, 2003). A window sequence of fixed length is used to capture a signal section, resulting in a fixed spectral resolution. The STFT is applied on windowed sections of the signal thus providing an analysis profile at regular time instances. However, the STFT can provide only averaged frequency information of the signal and it lacks the flexibility of arbitrary time-frequency localization (Polikarg, online, 2006). Such a rigid analysis regime is in striking contrast with the unpredictably dynamic spectral-temporal profile of information-carrying audio signals. Instead, signal characteristics would be analyzed and represented more accurately by a more versatile description providing a time-frequency multi-resolution pertinent to the signal dynamics. The approaches included in the MPEG 1 standard and elsewhere allow the switching between two different analysis window sizes depending on the value of the signal entropy (ISO/IEC 11172-3, 1993), or the changes in the estimated signal variance (Lincoln, 1998). Greater flexibility, however, is needed. The wavelet transform presents an attractive alternative by providing frequency-dependent resolution, which can better match the hearing mechanism (Polikarg,online, 2006). Specifically, long windows analyze low frequency components and achieve high frequency resolution while progressively shorter windows analyze higher frequency components to achieve better time resolution. Wavelet analysis has found numerous signal processing applications including video and image compression (Abbate et al., 2002; Jaffard et.al., 2001), perceptual audio coding (Veldhuis et. al., 1998), high quality audio compression and psychoacoustic model approximation (Sinha and Tewfik, 1993).

Wavelet-based approaches have been previously proposed for perceptual audio coding. Sinha et al. (1993) used the masking model proposed in (Veldhuis et. al.,

1998) to first calculate masking thresholds in the frequency domain by using the fast Fourier transform (FFT). Those thresholds were used to compute a reconstruction error constraint caused either by quantization or by the approximation of the wavelet coefficients used in the analysis. If the reconstruction errors were kept below those thresholds then no perceptual distortion was introduced. The constraints were then translated into the wavelet domain to ensure transparent wavelet audio coding.

Black et al. (1995) mimicked the critical bands distribution with a wavelet packet tree structure and directly calculated the signal energy and hearing threshold in the wavelet domain. This information was in turn used to compute masking profiles. Since the N-point FFT was no longer needed, the computational complexity was greatly reduced. Specifically, it was reported that the new method only requires 1/3 of the computational effort when compared to the MPEG 1 Layer 1 encoder.

In (Zurera, et. al., 2001), Zurera et al. presented a new algorithm to effectively translate psychoacoustic model information into the wavelet domain, even when low-selectivity filters were used to implement the wavelet transform or wavelet packet decomposition. They first calculated the masking and auditory thresholds in the frequency domain by using the Fourier transform. Based on several hypotheses (orthogonality of sub band signals and white noise-like quantization noise in each sub band), those thresholds were divided by the equivalent filter frequency response magnitude of the corresponding filter bank branch, forming the overall masking threshold in wavelet domain.

Carnero et al. (1999) constructed a wavelet domain psychoacoustic model representation using a frame- synchronized fast wavelet packet transform algorithm. Masking thresholds due to simultaneous frequency masking were estimated in a manner similar to (Cox, 1997). The energy in each sub band was calculated as the sum of the square of the wavelet coefficients, scaled by the estimated tonality and finally extended by a spreading function. Masking thresholds due to temporal masking were found by further considering the energy within each sub band. Final masking thresholds were obtained by considering both simultaneous and temporal masking as well as the band thresholds in absolute quiet. However, this model was tailored specifically for speech signals and its effectiveness on wideband audio remains untested.

The above psychoacoustic modeling methods are either computationally expensive (Zurera, et. al., 2001; Sinha and Tewfik, 1993; Veldhuis et. al., 1998; Reyes et. al., 2003) by relying on the Fourier transforms for the computation of the psychoacoustic model, or approximate the critical bands sub-optimally (Black and Zeytinoglu, 1995; Carnero et. al., 1999), which may result in objectionable audible distortion in the reconstructed signal. In contrast, it has been shown (Wu et. al., 2005) that the discrete wavelet transform (DWT) requires a significantly lower computational load when compared both to the discrete cosine transform (DCT) or the discrete

Fourier transform (DFT) while supporting psychoacoustically-based models, and therefore it still presents an attractive alternative.

In this chapter, we present a new psychoacoustic model in the wavelet domain. Wavelet analysis results are incorporated in effective simultaneous and temporal masking. Furthermore, the proposed model introduces a wavelet packet-based decomposition that better approximates critical bands distribution. The proposed model maintains perceptual transparency and provides an attractive alternative appropriate for audio compression and watermarking. A high quality audio coder utilizing the proposed psychoacoustic model is developed and compared with MP3 audio coder in next chapter. Experimental results show that the proposed audio coder performs better than the mp3 coder. It provides a better audio quality with the same bit rate or the same audio quality with less bit rate.

This chapter is organized as follows: In Section 8.2, we introduce the wavelet and relevant discrete packet transform that will be used for time-frequency analysis. In Section 8.3, we develop and present the improved psychoacoustic model based on wavelet analysis. Experimental evaluation results are included in Section 8.4. Conclusions are made in Section 8.5.

8.2 WAVELET TRANSFORM ANALYSIS

The Fourier transform and its fast implementations have provided a powerful spectral analysis tool. For time-varying signals, the short-time Fourier transform (STFT) is employed and it typically uses a time window of fixed length applied at regular intervals to obtain a portion of the signal assumed to be stationary. The resulting time-varying spectral representation is critical for non-stationary signal analysis, but in this case it comes at fixed spectral and temporal resolution. For audio, however, it is desired that the analysis provides good time resolution for high frequency and good frequency resolution for low frequency components (Polikarg, online, 2006). Wavelet analysis presents an attractive alternative by to the STFT by utilizing windows of variable width, which can effectively provide resolution of varying granularity. The length of the analysis window is inversely proportional to the frequency band being analyzed, thus applying short windows for high frequency components and longer windows for low frequency components. This provides multi-resolution information for the entire signal.

The continuous wavelet transform (CWT) of signal *s(t)* is defined as (Abbate et. al., 2002):

$$CWT(\alpha, \tau) = \frac{1}{\sqrt{\alpha}} \int s(t)\psi * (\frac{(t-\tau)}{\alpha})dt \tag{8.1}$$

where * is the complex conjugate operation, t is time, τ is the translation parameter, α is the scale parameter and $\psi(t)$ is the transforming function, called mother wavelet. Parameter τ provides the time location of the window and it varies as the window is shifted through the signal, while α controls the amount of stretching or compressing of the mother wavelet $\psi(\tau)$, which controls the shape of the wavelet.

In discrete time, signal $s(n)$ can be equivalently transformed by the discrete wavelet transform (DWT), which is discrete both in the time domain and the wavelet domain and it is defined as (Chan, 1995):

$$DWT(m, n) = 2^{\frac{-m}{2}} \sum_{k} s(k)\psi * (2^{-m}k - n) \tag{8.2}$$

This is the discrete version of equation (4.1), with $\tau=2^m n$ and $\alpha = 2m$, where m, n and k are integers.

The DWT is often implemented by a group of filter banks consisting of half-band high ($\pi/2$ to π) and low pass filters (0 to $\pi/2$). The signal is first divided into high and low frequency parts by the high and low pass filters respectively and the low frequency part is further decomposed into high and low frequency parts. The process continues on the low frequency part until the desired decomposition is achieved. Decomposition criteria are application-dependent and they may include target resolution, bandwidth and complexity. If both the high and low frequency parts are recursively decomposed, the DWT turns into the discrete wavelet packet transform (DWPT), which is a more flexible computational structure and it can be incorporated in audio analysis to closely approximate critical bands (Black and Zeytinoglu, 1995; Reyes et. al., 2003).

8.3 AN IMPROVED WAVELET-BASED PSYCHOACOUSTIC MODEL

This section includes the process of building the psychoacoustic model, and it presents an improved decomposition of the signal into 25 bands using the discrete wavelet packet transform (DWPT) to closely approximate the critical bands, followed by the implementation of temporal masking.

The proposed wavelet-based psychoacoustic model aims at a better spectral decomposition of the audio signal in order to closely mimic the human auditory system. Specifically, it provides a better approximation of the critical band partition and it considers both frequency and temporal masking effects for a more precise calculation of the masking thresholds. It will be shown that the proposed analysis procedure provides more space for inserting digital audio watermarks.

The general structure of the psychoacoustic model computation is illustrated in Figure 1 (Sinha and Tewfik, 1993; Black and Zeytinoglu, 1995; Zurera et al., 2001; Carnero et al., 1999).

The processing steps proceed as follows (He et al., 2006-a):

1.   The CD quality input audio is segmented into overlapped frames.
2.   Each frame is decomposed by the DWPT into 25 sub bands that approximate the auditory critical bands as illustrated in Figure 1.
3.   Signal energy in each band is computed in the wavelet domain to provide the Bark spectrum energy as.

$$E(z) = \sum_i x_i^2(z) \tag{8.3}$$

where z is the sub band index($1 \leq z \leq 25$) and x_i is the *ith* wavelet coefficient of the z sub band.

4.   Because noise and tone have different masking properties, the tonality is estimated in each band to determine the extent the signal in that band is noise-like or tone-like.

$$a(z) = \lambda a_{tmn}(z) + (1 - \lambda)a_{nmn}(z) \tag{8.4}$$

where $a(z)$ is the totality factor, $a_{tmn}(z)$ is the tone masking noise index calculated as

$$a_{tmn}(z) = -0.275z - 15.025 \tag{8.5}$$

a_{nmn} is noise-masking-noise index and is fixed as:

$$a_{nmn} = -9 \tag{8.6}$$

A Psychoacoustic Model Based on the Discrete Wavelet Packet Transform

Figure 1. Illustration of the psychoacoustic model computation

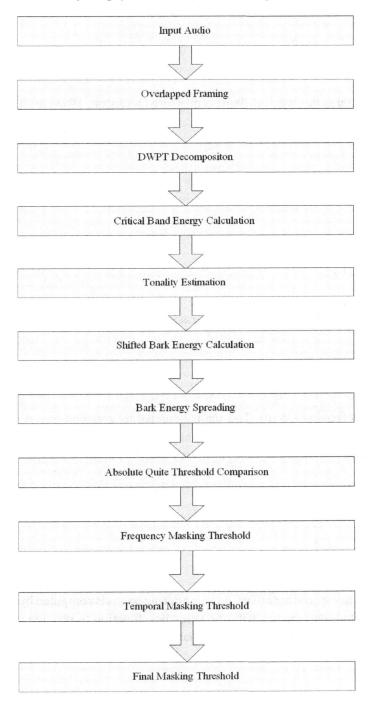

λ is a tonality coefficient parameter and calculated as

$$\lambda = \min(\frac{sfm}{sfm_{min}}, 1) \tag{8.7}$$

where *sfm* is the spectral flatness measure (Jonhston, 1998) in dB and calculated as

$$sfm = \frac{\mu_g}{\mu_a} \tag{8.8}$$

where

$$\mu_g = (\prod_{i=1}^{N} PSD_i)^{(1/N)} \tag{8.9}$$

is the geometric mean of the power spectral density (PSD) and

$$\mu_a = (\sum_{i=1}^{N} PSD_i) / N \tag{8.10}$$

sfm_{min} is fixed at -25 dB. The *sfm* is bounded by zero and one. A close to one *sfm* value means the signal has flat spectral and is noise-like. A close to zero *sfm* value, on the other hand, indicates tone-like signal.

5. Shifted bark energy is calculated by scaling the bark energy according to the tonality factor.

$$SE(z) = E(z)10^{\frac{a(z)}{10}} \tag{8.11}$$

6. The energy spreading effects on neighboring bands is computed by convolving the shifted bark energy with the spreading function to provide the effective masking threshold in each critical band.

$$C(z) = SE(z) * SP(z) \tag{8.12}$$

where SP(z) is the spreading function defined in MPEG 2 standard and * is convolution.

7. The masking threshold in each critical band is normalized by the band width and then compared with the threshold in absolute quiet. The maximum of the two is selected as the masking threshold.

$$T(z) = \max(\frac{C(z)}{L(z)}, T_{abs}(z)) \qquad (8.13)$$

where $L(z)$ is the length of sub band z and $T_{abs}(z)$ is the absolute threshold of hearing for sub band z.

8. Temporal masking threshold is calculated within each band. The frequency masking and temporal masking thresholds are compared. The final masking threshold for the particular signal frame is the maximum of the two as illustrated in Section 8.3.3.

As it can be seen in Figure 1, both temporal and spectral masking information are considered in the computation of the final masking threshold. In the introduced model temporal masking effects include both pre- and post-echo. However, in contrast to other approaches (e.g., D. Sinha and A.Tewfik, 1993) here the computation uses more precise critical bank approximations as well as simultaneous masking results obtained in the wavelet domain.

8.3.1 Signal Decomposition with the Discrete Wavelet Packet Transform (DWPT)

As mentioned in previous Section, the discrete wavelet packet transform (DWPT) can conveniently decompose the signal into a critical band-like partition (Sinha and Tewfik, 1993; Zurera et. al., 2001; Carnero et al., 1999). The standard critical bands are included in Chapter 1, Table 1. Table 1 in the current chapter lists the critical bands approximation used in alternative approaches (Liu, 2004; Carnero et al., 1999).

In this work, we divided the input audio signal into 25 sub bands using the DWPT in the manner shown in Figure 2, where the band index is enumerated from 1 to 25 to cover the complete audible spectrum (frequencies up to 22 kHz). The corresponding frequencies obtained by this DWPT decomposition are listed in Table 2.

As we will show in Section 8.3.2, this decomposition achieves a closer approximation of the standard critical bands than that used elsewhere (Liu, 2004;

Table 1. Alternative critical bands of alternative (Liu, 2004; Carnero, et al., 1999)

Critical Band Index	Lower Edge (Hz)	Center Edge (Hz)	Upper Edge (Hz)
1	0	43	86
2	86	129	172
3	172	215	258
4	258	301	344
5	344	386	430
6	430	473	516
7	516	602	689
8	689	774	861
9	861	946	1033
10	1033	1118	1205
11	1205	1290	1378
12	1378	1548	1722
13	1722	1893	2067
14	2067	2238	2411
15	2411	2582	2756
16	2756	3099	3445
17	3445	3788	4134
18	4134	4477	4823
19	4823	5166	5512
20	5512	6200	6890
21	6890	7578	8268
22	8268	9645	11025
23	11025	12402	13781
24	13781	15157	16537
25	16537	17915	19293
26	19293	20672	22050

Carnero et al., 1999), thus providing a more accurate psychoacoustic model computation.

The signal decomposition resulting from wavelet analysis needs to satisfy the spectral resolution requirements of the human auditory system, which match the critical bands distribution. On the other hand, the selection of the wavelet basis is critical for meeting

The required temporal resolution, which is less than 10 ms at high frequency areas and up to 100 ms at low frequency areas (Bosi and Goldberg, 2003). In order to have the appropriate analysis window size to accommodate that temporal resolution for wideband audio, we choose wavelet base of order 8 (length L = 16 samples) whose specific properties are as follows:

The frame length (in samples) at level j ($2 \leq j \leq 8$) is given by

$$F_j = 2^j \tag{8.14}$$

The duration of the analysis window (in samples) at level j is (Liu, 2004; Carnero, et. al., 1999)

Figure 2. DWPT-based signal decomposition

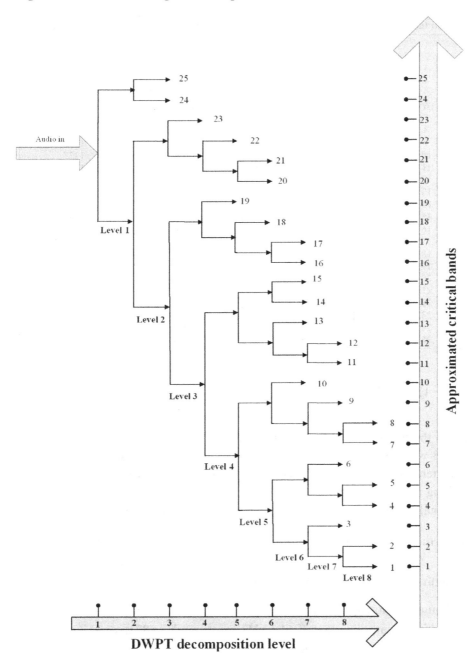

Table 2. Critical bands of proposed model

Critical Band Index	Lower Edge (Hz)	Center Edge (Hz)	Upper Edge (Hz)
1	0	43	86
2	86	129	172
3	172	258	344
4	344	387	430
5	430	473	516
6	516	602	687
7	687	730	773
8	773	816	859
9	859	945	1031
10	1031	1203	1375
11	1375	1462	1549
12	1549	1634	1719
13	1719	1891	2062
14	2062	2234	2406
15	2406	2578	2750
16	2750	2922	3093
17	3093	3265	3437
18	3437	3781	4125
19	4125	4813	5512
20	5512	5968	6437
21	6437	6906	7375
22	7375	8313	9250
23	9250	10137	11024
24	11024	13762	16538
25	16538	19294	22050

$$W_j = (L-1)(F_j - 1) + 1 \tag{8.15}$$

where L is the length of Daubechies filter coefficients (L = 16 in this case). The Daubechies wavelet is selected because it is the most compactly supported wavelet (finer frequency resolution) compared to other wavelet bases with the same number of vanishing moments (Daubechies, 1992).

For signal bandwidth of 22 kHz, the maximum frame length is $F_{max} = 2^8 = 256$ samples, which provides frequency resolution of $\dfrac{22kHz}{256} = 86Hz$. The minimum frame length is $F_{min} = 2^2 = 4$ samples with frequency resolution $\dfrac{22kHz}{4} = 5.5kHz$. The maximum duration of the analysis window is $W_{max} = 15 * (256 - 1) + 1 = 3826$ samples, which at sampling rate of 44.1 kHz corresponds to 87 ms and it applies to the low frequency end, while the minimum duration of the analysis window is $W_{min} = 15 * (4 - 1) + 1 = 46$ samples, or about 1 ms, which applies to the high frequency end.

8.3.2 Wavelet Decomposition Evaluation

While techniques based on the Fourier transform dominate in the implementation of psychoacoustic models, wavelet-based approaches are relatively new. In (Carnero et. al., 1999), frame-synchronized fast wavelet packet transform algorithms were used to decompose wideband speech into 21 sub bands, which approximate the critical bands. The spreading function used was optimized to speech listening. For wideband audio, Liu (2004) has extended that work and appropriately altered the spreading function in order to ensure transparency and inaudibility in audio watermarking applications. A similar critical bands partition was implemented, which in that case spanned the entire audible spectrum and consisted of 26 bands.

Table, Chapter 1, as well as Tables 1 and 2 in this chapter list the center frequencies and extent of standard critical bands (Cox, 1998), past model approaches (Liu, 2004; Carnero et al., 1999), and the proposed model, respectively. The degree to which the two different approaches approximate the standard critical bands partition can be examined by plotting the critical bands starting frequencies, as shown on Figure 3. When the differences in starting frequency are plotted as shown in Figure 4, it is readily observed that the proposed band partition is substantially closer to the standard, particularly beyond the 16th critical band (frequencies of 2800 Hz and higher). The differences between the two approaches are more striking when critical bands center frequency differences are examined, as depicted on Figure 5, where it can be seen that the proposed approach is considerably closer to the standard. A better approximation to the standard critical bands can provide a more accurate computation of the psychoacoustic model. While this wavelet approach yields a spectral partition that is much closer to the standard critical bands frequencies the inherent continuous subdivision of the spectrum by a factor of 2 prevents an exact match. However, the overall analysis features of this approach outlined elsewhere in this discussion uphold its overall appeal over competing techniques.

8.3.3 Window Size Switching and Temporal Masking

Temporal masking is observed before and after a strong signal (masker) has been switched on and off abruptly. If a weak signal (maskee) is present in the vicinity of the masker temporal masking may cause it to become inaudible even before the masker onset (pre-masking) or after the masker vanishes (post masking). Typically, the duration of pre-masking is less than one tenth that of the post-masking, which is in the order of 50 to 100 ms (Lincoln, 1998), depending on the masker amplitude.

Although pre-masking is relatively a short-time phenomenon, it has important implications and has had to be addressed in audio analysis and compression, par-

Figure 3. Starting frequencies (lower edge) of each critical band

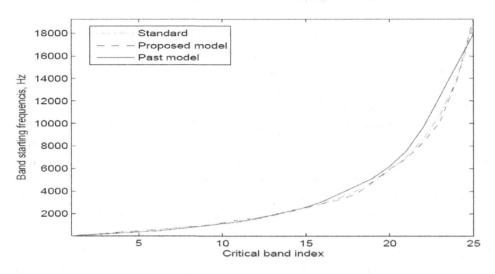

Figure 4. Starting frequencies (lower edge) differences for each critical band

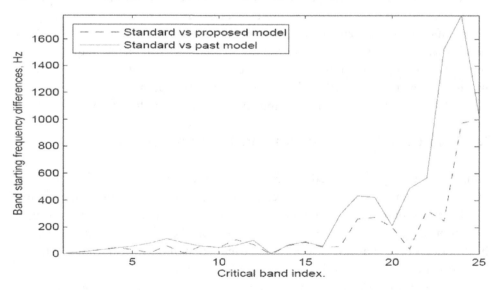

Figure 5. Center frequencies differences for each critical band

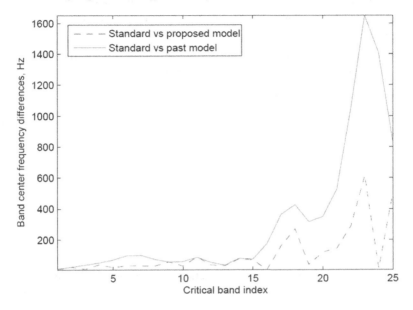

ticularly in minimizing the so-called pre-echo problem (Painter and Spanias, 2000; Bosi and Goldberg, 2003; Lincoln, 1998). A good way to mitigate this problem has been the use of adaptive analysis frame size. Analysis using long frame size requires less computation than shorter frame size, which is a critical aspect in real time applications and it can also yield lower bit rate in compression applications or higher watermarking capacity but at the risk of permitting audible distortion caused by large variations in the signal stationarity, such as the presence of an attack in only part of the frame (Sinha and Tewfik, 1993). Therefore, several approaches have been proposed for seamlessly switching between different frame sizes.

The proposed psychoacoustic model was tested on CD-quality audio (sampling rate of 44.1 kHz) with nominal analysis frame duration of 46 ms (2048 samples). While this frame size is adequate for slowly changing signal characteristics, it may be too long for rapidly changing signals. Consider for example the case that a silent period is followed by a percussive sound, such as from castanet or triangles within the same analysis block. In this case, quantization noise during the coding process will spread over the entire block and it will be audible in the portion before the signal attack. Pre-masking effects will be unable to cover the offending pre-echo noise in its entirety, which will therefore become audible (Sinha and Tewfik, 1993).

Window size switching is used to address pre-echo effects and in the proposed model it proceeds as follows:

1. The input signal is divided into frames of 2048 samples with 50% overlap.
2. Each frame is decomposed into 25 sub bands using the DWPT method outlined in Section 8.3.1.
3. The wavelet coefficients x_i are normalized by dividing each coefficient with the maximum absolute coefficient in the frame

$$x_i = \frac{x_i}{\max(|x_i|)} \tag{8.16}$$

4. The normalized wavelet energy entropy of the frame is calculated

$$E = -\sum_{i=a}^{b} x_i^2 \log_2 x_i^2 \tag{8.17}$$

where a and b are the starting and ending locations of the analysis frame containing the wavelet coefficients.

5. If the change of E from the previous frame to the present frame exceeds a certain threshold then the frame is switched to a frame of half the size. In this approach, the initial 2048 samples frame is switched to three 1024 samples long frames with 50% overlap.
6. The change of the energy entropy of the new 1024 samples frames is calculated using Equation (8.5) and (8.6). Exceeding a threshold will again result in a further switching step, which divides each 1024 samples frame into three 512 samples frames with 50% overlap.
7. Further frame switching to 256 samples is permissible and it may occur in some extreme transient signals. Beyond that point no subsequent switching is performed and the switching process is terminated.

The post masking effect is also considered in this psychoacoustic model by implementing an approach similar to (Lincoln, 1998). However, this time the entire algorithm operates in the wavelet domain.

$$T^p(i) = \lambda T^p(i-1) + (1-\lambda)T^s(i) \tag{8.18}$$

where i is the frame (time) index, λ is a control factor with value between 0 and 1, $T^p(i)$ and $T^p(i-1)$ are the temporal masking thresholds for the current and previous frame, respectively and $T^s(i)$ is the frequency (simultaneous) masking threshold derived by the proposed DWPT as described in Section 8.3. The derived masking threshold is provided by

$$T = \max(T^s(i), T^p(i)) \qquad\qquad (8.19)$$

Note that in Equation (8.7) factor λ controls how much the previous frame temporal masking threshold and the current frequency masking threshold contribute to the current temporal masking threshold. A greater λ denotes stronger temporal masking effects and therefore a slower masker decay slope. A smaller λ on the other hand, denotes weaker temporal masking effects and a steeper masker decay slope.

8.4 EXPERIMENTAL PROCEDURES AND RESULTS

In this section, the proposed DWPT-based psychoacoustic model will be compared to the perceptual entropy model most commonly used, which has provided the basis for the widely used MP3 standard (ISO/IEC 11172-3, 1993; Cox, 1997), and others, from two useful perspectives: (1) the extent to which portions of the signal power spectrum can be rendered inaudible and therefore removed without audibly perceived impact and (2) the amount of reduction in the sum of signal-to-masking ratio (SSMR) that can be achieved, which is a direct indication of the degree the coding bit rate can be lowered in compression applications without further loss in perceived quality.

8.4.1 Masking of the Power Spectrum

Psychoacoustic analysis of audible signals in the frequency domain can provide the simultaneous masking threshold. Key parameters used in this analysis are the specific distribution of signal components, the spreading function that provides the overall extent of the masking effect and the tonal quality of signal components. Spectral components below the masking threshold are inaudible.

The original audio signal example in time domain is shown in Figure 6 and its short-time analysis example is shown in Figure 7. There, the power spectral density of an audio frame (46.44 ms of audio at 44.1 kHz sampling rate) is depicted (obtained by the square of the magnitude of the DFT coefficients), together with the resulting masking threshold, denoted by the solid line, which was derived according to the perceptual entropy (PE) model used in the MPEG-1 psychoacoustical model 2 (ISO/IEC 11172-3, 1993; Cox, 1997). The power spectrum is divided into two areas, A, which is the set of spectral regions where the power spectrum exceeds the masking

Figure 6. Analysis of a signal frame in time domain

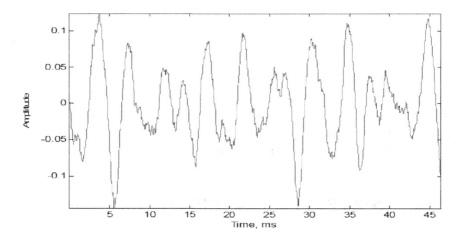

threshold, and B, the collection of all other areas. In general audio, these regions are continuous in the frequency domain (no widely separate spectral components.) Region B is the inaudible part of the spectrum and may be removed without any perceived effect, provided the overall signal loudness is maintained.

If the DFT order is L and the number of the components below the masking threshold (Region B) is R (R/2 in the positive and R/2 in the negative parts of the spectrum) then the portion of the removable spectrum is given by

$$Wmc = \frac{R}{L} * 100\%$$

(8.20)

The same audio signal frame was analyzed using the proposed technique. The wavelet power spectrum is obtained by squaring the magnitude of the wavelet coefficients, and it is shown in Figure 8, together with the associated masking threshold obtained using the procedure outlined in Section 8.3.

Note in Figure 7 and 8, the frequency is in linear scale and normalized to 1. From Figures 7 and 8 it can be seen that for this particular audio frame substantially more spectral components fall under the masking threshold and are therefore inaudible than in the Fourier-based analysis. The percentage of wavelet spectral components that falls below the audible spectrum is computed in a manner similar to that of the DFT power spectrum.

Figure 7. Analysis of a signal frame using the PE model (Cox, 1998)

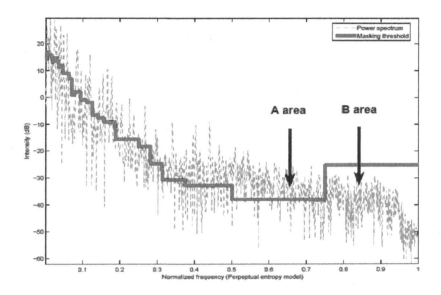

Figure 8. Analysis of a signal frame using the proposed DWPT-based model

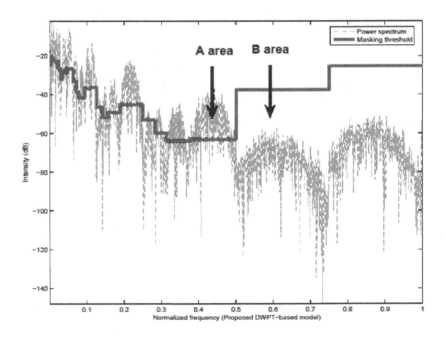

A set of five audio files was used to evaluate and compare the proposed and the standard analysis methods. They contained varying musical pieces of CD-quality that included jazz, classical, pop, country and rock music, each about 20 seconds long. The percentage of the removable power spectrum was computed and the results are included in Table 3. As it can be seen, the overall gain in the extent of masked regions provided by the proposed wavelet method is 22%.

We also compared the average inaudible spectrum (IS) in each critical band and the results are shown in Figure 9.

Figure 9(a) is the average IS in each critical band calculated from PE model and Figure 9(b) is the average IS obtained from the proposed DWPT model, in dB for both cases, resulting from the analysis of the same audio material. Figure 9(c) shows the IS improvement, in dB, of DWPT over PE model in each critical band.

Supposing that the average amount of IS in critical band j derived from PE model is ISP_j and the amount of IS in the same critical band from DWPT model is ISD_j, then the IS improvement in jth critical band (ISI_j) of DWPT over PE model is defined as:

$$ISI_j = 10 \times \log 10(\frac{ISD_j}{ISP_j}) \tag{8.21}$$

A positive ISI_j means DWPT model provides more amount of IS in critical band j and a negative ISI_j on the other hand, means PE model provides more IS in that critical band.

As we can see from Figure 9(c), DWPT outperforms PE model in critical bands 18 and above, thus providing more IS for frequencies above 3400 Hz.

Subjective listening tests were conducted as well, and confirmed that by removing the masked spectral components the processed audio signals are indistinguishable to the original for both the MPEG-based and the proposed technique.

Table 3. Average power spectrum portion under masking threshold (Cox, 1998)

Audio Type	PE Model (%)	Proposed DWPT-based Model (%)	Gain (%)
Country	51	73	22
Jazz	47	74	27
Pop	57	74	17
Rock	67	76	9
Classic	44	78	34
AVERAGE	53	75	22

8.4.2 Signal-to-Masking Ratio Reduction

The other useful consideration in comparing the effectiveness of the two methods is their ability to facilitate lower bit rates in compression schemes. The signal-to-masking ratio (SMR) plays an important role in this process because it is a measure of how high the quantization noise floor can be allowed to raise in the audible signal components. A small SMR indicates that a relatively high noise floor is permissible and therefore fewer bits may be used for coding. The performance metric that captures this effect for the entire spectrum of a particular analysis frame is defined as the average sum of the signal-to-masking ratio (SSMR).

Specifically, if S is the power spectrum of the signal, M is the masking threshold and N is the quantization noise introduced in the audio coding process, all in dB and functions of frequency, then the signal-to-masking ratio (SMR) is defined as

$$SMR = S - M \qquad (8.22)$$

Figure 9. Inaudible spectrum (IS) per critical band comparison

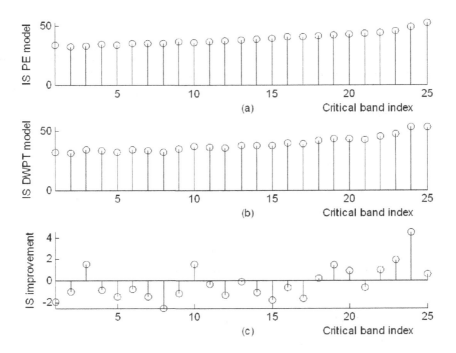

the signal-to-noise ratio (SNR) is defined as

$$SNR = S - N \qquad (8.23)$$

and the noise-to-mask ratio (NMR) is defined as

$$NMR = N - M \qquad (8.24)$$

or

$$NMR = SMR - SNR \qquad (8.25)$$

Negative *NMR* denotes that the noise power is below the masking threshold and therefore it remains inaudible. In audio compression, reducing the SMR results in lower coding bit rate by allowing larger quantization noise to be tolerated.

The lower bound estimate for the perceptual coding of audio signals based on the psychoacoustic model is the perceptual entropy (PE) and it is defined as (Bosi and Goldberg, 2003):

$$PE = \frac{1}{L} \sum_{i=1}^{L} \max\{0, \frac{1}{2} \log_2(\frac{Ps_i}{Pm_i})\} \qquad (8.26)$$

where L is the number of samples in the audio signal, Ps_i and Pm_i are the intensity of the signal and masking threshold of the *ith* sample, respectively.

Considering the following relationship pair $S=10\log10P_s$ and $M=10\log10P_m$ as well as Equation (8.10), we can rewrite Equation (8.14) as:

$$PE =$$

$$\frac{1}{L} \sum_{i=1}^{L} \max\{0, \frac{1}{2} \log_2(\frac{10^{\frac{S_i}{10}}}{10^{\frac{M_i}{10}}})\} = \frac{1}{L} \sum_{i=1}^{L} \max\{0, \frac{1}{2} \log_2(10^{\frac{SMR_i}{10}})\} \qquad (8.27)$$

From Equation (8.15), it can be seen that the reduction of SMR (as long as SMR is greater than 0) will lead to the reduction in PE and consequently a lower bit rate for audio coding by allowing larger quantization noise to be tolerated.

Examining the analysis of the previous example depicted in Figure 6 and 7, areas A and B can be defined in terms of SMR as A = {S|SM R >= 0} and B = {S|SM R < 0}. In audio compression applications, in area A, which consumes all allocated bits, the encoded signal must be close enough to the original signal to maintain the quantization noise below the masking threshold.

Let SMR_i denote the SMR of the *ith* sample of area A in the power spectrum or the power wavelet spectrum in the *jth* signal frame, Lj denote the length of A area in that frame and G be the number of total frames in the signal analyzed. Then the sum of SMR (SSMR) in dB for the duration of the signal is given by:

$$SSMR = \sum_{j=1}^{G} \sum_{i=1}^{L_j} SMR_{i,j}$$
(8.28)

The average SMR is defined as

$$SMR_{avg} = \frac{SSMR}{K}$$
(8.29)

where K is the total number of samples in the signal.

The two models, proposed and standard were compared using the same audio material as in the previous test. The results are summarized in Table 4.

As it can be seen from Table 4, in the proposed wavelet-based technique the SSMR was reduced by as much as **86%** (for country music), while the average reduction rate reaches 57%, indicating that a significant decrease in coding bit rate is possible.

We then compared the average SSMR in each critical band obtained from the analysis of the same audio material and the results are shown in Figure 10.

Figure 10(a) shown the average SSMR in dB in each critical band calculated from the PE model and Figure 10(b) is the average SSMR got from the proposed DWPT model. Figure 10(c) shows the SSMR improvement in dB of the DWPT over the PE model in each critical band.

Supposing that the average amount of SSMR in critical band *j* derived from PE model is $SSMRP_j$ and the amount of IS in the same critical band from DWPT model is $SSMRD_j$, then the SSMR improvement in *jth* critical band ($SSMRI_j$) of DWPT over PE model is defined as:

Table 4. Sum of signal-to masking ratio comparison

Audio Type	PE Model (dB)	DWPT-based Model Model (dB)	SMR Reduction (%)
Country	17178	7129	59
Jazz	16108	5447	66
Pop	20061	12156	40
Rock	21266	14411	32
Classic	14756	2075	86
AVERAGE	17874	8244	57

$$SSMRI_j = 10 \times \log 10(\frac{SSMRP_j}{SSMRD_j}) \qquad (8.29)$$

A positive $SSMRI_j$ means the DWPT model results in a lower sum of signal to masking ratio (SSMR) in critical band j compared to PE model, which is desirable for audio watermarking. A negative $SSMRI_j$ on the other hand, means PE model performs better than DWPT model in *jth* critical band in terms of SSMR.

From Figure 10(c) we can see all the values are positive which demonstrates a better performance of DWPT model for the entire audible spectrum.

8.5 CONCLUSION

We have constructed a novel psychoacoustic model, which can be applicable to audio compression and watermarking. This model uses the discrete wavelet packet transform to provide multi-resolution analysis that closely mimics auditory processing and it is superior to Fourier transform-based techniques both from the computational as well as the resolution perspectives. The auditory critical bands distribution is implemented more accurately than in previous techniques. The model includes simultaneous and temporal masking effects, all computed in the wavelet domain. Experiments conducted on a wide variety of audio signals demonstrate that the proposed method provides broader masking capabilities thus revealing that larger signal regions are in fact inaudible and therefore removable without noticeable effect, a fact that was confirmed in listening tests. The masked regions may be ignored in audio compression thus resulting in lower information rates or used for hiding more information in audio watermarking. Furthermore, the signal-to-masking ratio is further reduced indicating that in coding applications this approach can lead to further bit rate reduction without quality degradation.

Figure 10. Sum of signal to masking ratio (SSMR) per critical band comparison

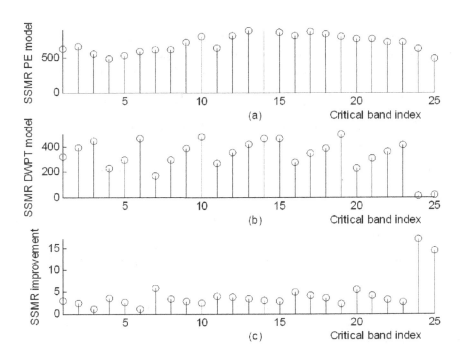

Based on this psychoacoustic model, we will present a high quality perceptual audio codec in the next chapter which employs a similar structure to MPEG I layer III (MP3), including quantization and Huffman coding. The evaluation of this perceptual audio codec shows that the proposed audio codec achieves transparency coding and outperforms the MP3 codec by providing better audio quality with same bit rates.

REFERENCES

Abbate, A., Decusatis, C. M., & Das, P. K. (2002). *Wavelets and subbands, fundamentals and applications*. Boston, MA: Birkhauser.

Black, M., & Zeytinoglu, M. (1995). Computationally efficient wavelet packet coding of wide-band stereo signals. In *Proceedings of the IEEE International Conference on Acoustics, Speech and Signal Processing (ICASSP)* (pp. 3075-3078). Detroit, MI.

Bosi, M., & Goldberg, R. E. (2003). *Introduction to digital audio coding and standards*. Norwell, MA: Kluwer Academic Publishers.

Carnero, B., & Drygajlo, A. (1999). Perceptual speech coding and enhancement using frame-synchronized fast wavelet packet transform algorithms. *IEEE Transactions on Signal Processing, 47*(6), 1622–1635. doi:10.1109/78.765133

Chan, Y. T. (1995). *Wavelet basics*. Norwell, MA: Kluwer Academic Publishers.

Cox, I. J., Miller, M. L., & Bloom, J. A. (2002). *Digital watermarking*. San Francisco, CA: Academic Press.

Daubechies, I. (1992). Ten lectures on wavelets. *CBMS-NSF Regional Conference Series in Applied Mathematics, 61*.

ISO/IEC, 11172-3 (1993). Coding of moving picture and associated audio for digital storage media at up to about 1.5 Mbits - part 3 audio.

Jaffard, S., Meyer, Y., & Ryan, R. D. (2001). *Wavelets tools for science and technology*. Philadelphia, PA: SIAM.

Johnston, J. D. (1998). Transform coding of audio signals using perceptual noise criteria. *IEEE Journal on Selected Areas in Communications, 6*(2), 314–323. doi:10.1109/49.608

Lincoln, B. (1998). An experimental high fidelity perceptual audio coder. *Project in MUS420* Retrieved from http://www-ccrma.stanford.edu /jos/bosse/

Liu, Q. (2004). *Digital audio watermarking utilizing discrete wavelet packet transform*. (Unpublished Master's thesis). Chaoyang University of Technology, Taiwan, China.

Painter, T., & Spanias, A. (2000). Perceptual coding of digital audio. *Proceedings of the IEEE, 88*(4), 451–513. doi:10.1109/5.842996

Pan, D. (1995). A tutorial on mpeg/audio compression. *IEEE MultiMedia, 2*(2), 60–74. doi:10.1109/93.388209

Polikarg, R. (2006). The wavelet tutorial. Retrieved from http://users.rowan.edu/polikar/Wavelets /wtpart1.html.

Reyes, N. R., Zurera, M. R., Ferreras, F. L., & Amores, P. J. (2003). Adaptive wavelet-packet analysis for audio coding purposes. *Signal Processing, 83*, 919–929. doi:10.1016/S0165-1684(02)00489-9

Sinha, D., & Tewfik, A. (1993). Low bit rate transparent audio compression using adapted wavelets. *IEEE Transactions on Signal Processing, 41*(12), 3463–3479. doi:10.1109/78.258086

Swanson, M. D., Zhu, B., Tewfik, A. H., & Boney, L. (1998). Robust audio watermarking using perceptual masking. *Elsevier Signal Processing, Special Issue on Copyright Protection and Access Control, 66*(3), 337–355.

Veldhuis, R. N. J., Breeuwer, M., & Van Der Wall, R. G. (1989). Subband coding of digital audio signals. *Philips Journal of Research, 44*(2/3), 329–343.

Wu, S., Huang, J., Huang, D., & Shi, Y. Q. (2005). Efficiently self-synchronized audio watermarking for assured audio data transmission. *IEEE Transactions on Broadcasting, 51*(1), 69–76. doi:10.1109/TBC.2004.838265

Zurera, M. R., Ferreras, F. L., Amores, M. P. J., Bascon, S. M., & Reyes, N. R. (2001). A new algorithm for translating psychoacoustic information to the wavelet domain. *Signal Processing, 81*, 519–531. doi:10.1016/S0165-1684(00)00230-9

Chapter 9
A High Quality Audio Coder Using Proposed Psychoacoustic Model

In order to show the application of the previous proposed psychoacoustic model in audio coding, we will develop in this chapter a high quality audio coder using the proposed psychoacoustic model from the previous chapter and compare this audio coder with the standard MP3 audio coder. As can be seen later in the experiment section, the proposed audio codec is preferred over the MP3 codec at the same compression bit rate, thus providing a potential usage for many audio applications.

9.1. STRUCTURE OF PROPOSED PERCEPTUAL AUDIO CODER

The structure of the proposed high quality perceptual audio encoder is shown in Figure 1 (He et al., 2008b). Input PCM audio samples are fed into the encoder. The time to frequency mapping creates a sub-sampled representation of the audio samples

DOI: 10.4018/978-1-61520-925-5.ch009

Figure 1. Structure of perceptual audio encoder

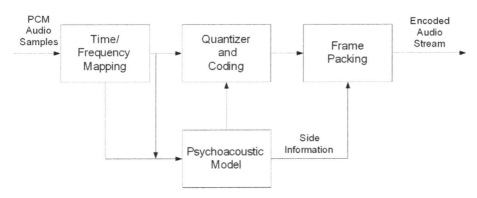

using the DWPT. The psychoacoustic model calculates the masking thresholds, which are later employed to control the quantizer and coding. Bit allocation strategy is utilized to allocate bits to each sub-band sample according to its perceptual importance. Typically, more bits are reserved for low frequency samples, which are perceptually more important. Quantization is performed in a way to keep the quantization noise below the audible threshold for transparent audio coding. The bit allocation information is transmitted together with the encoded audio as ancillary data or side information, which are used in the audio decoder to reconstruct the PCM audio samples. Lossless coding, which is usually Huffman coding, is employed to further remove the redundancy of the quantized value. The frame packing block packs the output of quantizer and coding block as well as the side information and yields the encoded audio stream.

Figure 2 shows the decoder of the proposed audio coding scheme. The encoded audio stream is fed into the frame unpacking block, which unpacks the compressed audio stream into the quantized samples as well as the side information. In the de-quantization and decoding block, Huffman decoding is performed first followed by de-quantization, using the side information extracted from the frame-unpacking block. The output is the audio samples in the wavelet domain, which are later transformed in time domain by the inverse time/frequency mapping block to form the decoded PCM audio samples.

Time/frequency mapping block and psychoacoustic model block are illustrated in chapter 7 as the proposed psychoacoustic model, so only quantizer and coding block is explained in the following section.

Figure 2. Structure of perceptual audio decoder

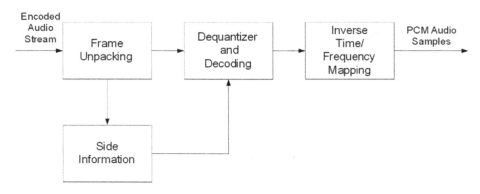

9.2 QUANTIZATION AND HUFFMAN CODING

The quantization and Huffman coding employed in the proposed audio codec is similar to that of the MPEG 1 layer III standard. The input to the quantization and Huffman coding block includes the spectral values (wavelet coefficients) of the frame, the maximum number of bits available for Huffman coding, the critical band partition table and the allowed distortion in each critical band (also called scalefactor band in audio coding).

The maximum number of bits available for Huffman coding for one frame (called granule in audio coding) is defined as

$$\max\_bits = \frac{bit\_rate * granule\_size}{sampling\_frequency} \qquad (9.1)$$

where *bit_rate* is the actual bit rate, *granul_size* is the number of spectral values in one granule (1024 for our case) and the sampling frequency is 44.1 kHz for CD quality audio.

The allowed distortion in each scalefactor band is calculated as

$$x\min(sb) = \frac{thrn(sb)}{bw(sb)} \qquad (9.2)$$

Table 1. Scalefactor band partition (sampling frequency 44.1 kHz)

Scalefactor band(*sb*)	Bandwidth(*bw*)	Index of start	Index of end
1	4	1	4
2	4	5	8
3	8	9	16
4	4	17	20
5	4	21	24
6	8	25	32
7	4	33	36
8	4	37	40
9	8	41	48
10	16	49	64
11	8	65	72
12	8	73	80
13	16	81	96
14	16	97	112
15	16	113	128
16	16	129	144
17	16	145	160
18	32	161	192
19	64	193	256
20	32	257	288
21	32	289	320
22	64	321	384
23	128	385	512
24	256	513	768
25	256	769	1024

where sb is the scalefactor band index, $thrn(sb)$ is the masking threshold estimated by proposed psychoacoustic model, and $bw(sb)$ is the bandwidth of each scalefactor band and can be read from Table 1.

Initialization process takes place first before the actual quantization. During this process,

1. The step size counter *qquant* and multiplication factor *scalefac_scale* are set to zero.

2. The initial value of the variable *quantaf* is set by the following equation:

$$quantaf = system\_const * \log_e(sfm) \tag{9.3}$$

where *sfm* is the spectral flatness measure given by:

$$sfm = \frac{e^{\frac{1}{n}(\sum_{i=0}^{n-1} \log xr(i)^2)}}{\frac{1}{n}\sum_{i=0}^{n-1} xr(i)^2} \tag{9.4}$$

here *n* is the number of spectral values, n = 1024 and *xr(i)* is the magnitude of the *ith* sample of the granule. The addition of *quantaf* and *qquant* called *global_gain*) controls the quantizer step size and ultimately controls the bit rate. The parameter *system_const* in Equation (9.3) is a system constant and empirically set to 10. This value ensures a faster termination of quantization process by using as many as possible the available bits at the first call of the quantization loop, resulting the a higher than desired bit sum.

3. The initial values of scalefactors within each scalefactor band are set to zero. Those values are later used to control noise allocation.

After the initialization process, two iteration loops are utilized in the quantization and coding block. One is the outer iteration loop, which controls the distortion and the other is inner iteration loop, which controls the bit rate.

The flow chart of the quantization iteration loops are illustrated in Figure 3 (outer loop) and Figure 4 (inner loop). The inner loop does the actual quantization, chooses the Huffman coding table and selects the quantization step size. The spectral values are non-uniformly quantized, the basic quantization formula is the same as that defined in MPEG-1/Audio standard:

$$is(i) = n\,\text{int}((\frac{|xr(i)|}{\sqrt[4]{2}^{qquant+quantaf}})^{0.75} - 0.0946) \tag{9.5}$$

Figure 3. Outer loop

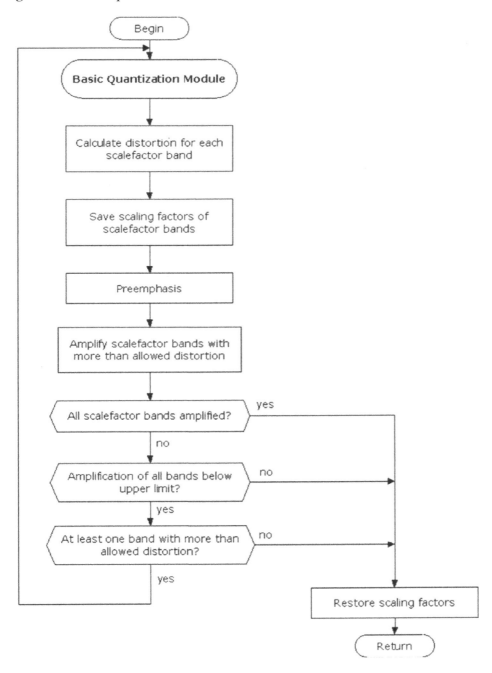

Figure 4. Inner loop of encoder

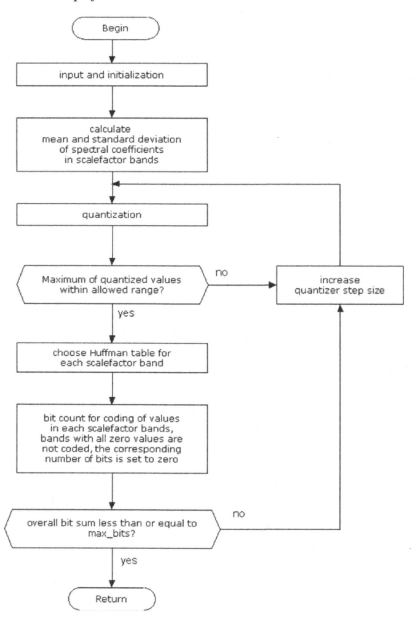

where

$|xr(i)|$=absolute value of sp*ectral line at index i*
*n*int =*nearest integer function*
is(*i*)=quantized absolu*te value at index i*

The maximum allowed quantized value is limited by the Huffman table size. If the current bit sum exceeds the desired bits, the quantizer step size is increased by *qquant=qquant*+1 until the maxim of the quantized value is within the range of Huffman code table.

Huffman coding is done with a similar way to MPEG I layer III standard.

The outer loop controls the quantization noise produced by the inner loop. The distortion produced by inner loop is measured within each scalefactor band and is given by

$$
xfsf(sb) =
$$

$$
\sum_{i=lbl(sb)}^{lbl(sb)+bw(sb)-1} \frac{(\mid xr(i) \mid -is(i)^{4/3} \times \sqrt[4]{2}^{qquant+quantaf})^2}{bandwidth(sb)} \tag{9.6}
$$

where $xr(i)$ is the spectral value and $is(i)$ is the quantized value of it, i is the sample index. The variable $\sqrt[4]{2}^{qquant+quantaf}$ is the quantizer step size *qstep*, *lbl*(*sb*) is the index of start in scalefactor band *sb*, its value can be found in Table 1 column 3. *bw*(*sb*) is the number of coefficients within scalefactor band *sb* and is given by Table 1 column 2. The bandwidth of each scalefactor band, *bandwidth*(*sb*), is derived from *bw*(*sb*), the total number of coefficients in one granule (1024) and the Nyquist frequency of PCM audio signal. The value of *bandwidth*(*sb*) is given by:

$$
bandwidth(sb) =
$$
$$
\frac{bw(sb) * Nyquist\_frequency}{granule\_size} \tag{9.7}
$$

The amplification of spectral value is controlled by scaling factors of each scalefactor band. Those scaling factors are saved temporarily in case the outer loop is cancelled without reaching a proper result. Those factors and the quantized values are transmitted to the decoder, giving an approximation.

When the quantization distortion exceeds the masking threshold measured by the psychoacoustic model, the amplification of spectral values is needed. By amplifying all the spectral values of the scalefactor bands where the masking requirements are violated, the quantization noise is therefore colored (shaped) to fit the varying frequency contours of the masking thresholds. The coloring of the noise is done by multiplication of all spectral values within scalefactor bands with the actual scaling factors before quantization. The multiplication is defined as:

$$xr(i) = xr(i) * \sqrt{2}^{((1+scalefac\_scale)*scalefactor(sb))} \tag{9.8}$$

where $xr(i)$ is the spectral value and i is the index. The variable *scalefactor(sb)* is the scaling factor in scalefactor band *sb*. The scalefactor multiplication factor *scalefac_scale* is initialized to zero before first iteration. If after some iterations the maximum number of the scaling factors would be exceeded, then the value of *scalefac_scale* is increase to 1 thus increasing the possible dynamic range of scaling factors. In this case, the actual scaling factors and spectral values have to be corrected accordingly.

The loops (outer and inner) terminate when any of the following conditions is true:

1. There is no scalefactor band with more than allowed distortion
2. All scalefactor bands are already amplified.
3. The amplification of at least one band exceeds the upper limit determined by the scalefactors.

9.3 EVALUATION OF PROPOSED AUDIO CODER

In this section, we will discuss some subjective tests that we have conducted to evaluate the quality of the audio encoded with the proposed audio perceptual coder. We discuss the material of the test audio first and present the testing results after that.

9.3.1 Test Audio

Eight audio files used in subjective listening tests are listed in Table 2. They are mono 16 bit CD-quality audio at 44.1 kHZ sampling rate. Note they include some audio signals like drum, castanets, etc. which are usually considered challenging to encode (Sinha and Tewfik, 1993). Those signals tend to cause pre-echo phenomena and introduce audible distortion into the encoded audio.

Table 2. Test audio files used in subjective listening tests

Audio Number	Instrument/Style
1	drum with orchestra
2	solo flute
3	solo castanets
4	solo castanets
5	solo harps
6	solo horn
7	violin with orchestra
8	solo trumpet

9.3.2 Subjective Listening Tests

A total of 11 people participated in our subjective listening tests. Most of them were young students with acute listening and some of them were researchers in the Digital Audio and Speech Processing lab with knowledge of audio psychoacoustic model, audio compression, audible distortion and listening test.

For subjective evaluation, double blind listening test was used because it was one of the most acclaimed methods of comparing codec quality. In this test, the listener (participant) compared various encoded sample audio against each other without knowing the source codec of each sample audio, which guarantees no psychological bias towards those codecs.

Our goals of the experiments were to test the transparency of the proposed codec and its performance compared to MP3 codec. A total of two different listening tests were performed. The first aimed at testing the codec transparency and the second was used for comparison purposes.

For each listening test, there are eight pairs of audio samples which are either original uncompressed music or encoded by different codec. The participants have no prior knowledge of the originality of the audio samples, i.e. they do not know whether those audio pieces are original or compressed by some audio codec, thus achieving double blind tests. The participants are asked to listen to each pair and give their preference to the one that has a better overall audio quality. Since the differences for some pairs are minor, a "not sure" response is permitted. The method we employed to deal with "not sure" response is explained as follows:

If for instance, x people prefer audio A, y people prefer audio B and z people give "not sure" response, then, the likelihood that people prefer audio A is given by:

Table 3. Transparency test DWPTC 64 kbits/s vs. original audio

Audio Number	Average Probability of Original Audio Preferred over DWPTC	Comments
1	56.2%	Transparent
2	50%	Transparent
3	64.2%	Nearly Transparent
4	64.2%	Nearly Transparent
5	68.7%	Original Preferred
6	44.4%	Transparent
7	37.6%	DWPTC Preferred
8	50%	Transparent

$$pre\_a = \frac{x+z}{x+z+y+z} \times 100\% = \frac{x+z}{x+y+2z} \times 100\% \tag{9.9}$$

During the first listening test, those eight audio files are encoded by the proposed audio codec (DWPTC) at 64 kbits/s and compared with the original uncompressed pairs. The results are listed in Table 3.

During the second listening test, the same eight audio files are encoded by the DWPTC and MPEG I layer III (MP3) codec (ISO/IEC, 11172-3, 1993) both at 64 kbits/s bit rate. The comparison results are shown in Table 4.

Note in each table, the first column is the test audio number, the second column is the average percentage of original audio (Table 3) or MP3 compressed audio (Table 4) preference over DWPTC and the third column is the evaluation. If the

Table 4. Codec comparison test DWPTC 64 kbits/s vs. MP3 at 64 kbits/s

Audio Number	Average Probability of MP3 Preferred over DWPTC	Comments
1	50%	Same Quality
2	53.3%	Same Quality
3	57.1%	Same Quality
4	53.8%	Same Quality
5	37.3%	DWPTC Preferred
6	37.5%	DWPTC Preferred
7	43.7%	Same Quality
8	50%	Same Quality

preference percentage is close to 0.5, then it is considered "transparent" for the first listening tests or "same quality" for the second test.

As we can see from Table 3, audio encoded by DWPTC at 64 kbits/s bit rate provides transparent or nearly transparent coding for all but one audio source compared to the original audio. From Table 4, the DWPTC outperforms the MP3 codec in two audio sources and provides same audio quality for the other 6 audio sources.

Although the trial size of our listening tests is relatively small, which gives limited confidence level, the results still shows that the proposed DWPTC is preferred over the MP3 codec at the same compression bit rate, thus providing a potential usage for many audio applications.

9.4 CONCLUSION

We have constructed in chapter 3 a novel psychoacoustic model which can be applicable to audio compression and watermarking. This model uses the discrete wavelet packet transform to provide multi-resolution analysis that closely mimics auditory processing and it is superior to Fourier transform-based techniques both from the computational as well as the resolution perspectives. The auditory critical bands distribution is implemented more accurately than in previous techniques. The model includes simultaneous and temporal masking effects, all computed in the wavelet domain. Experiments conducted on a wide variety of audio signals demonstrate that the proposed method provides broader masking capabilities thus revealing that larger signal regions are in fact inaudible and therefore removable without noticeable effect, a fact that was confirmed in listening tests. The masked regions may be ignored in audio compression thus resulting in lower information rates or used for hiding more information in audio watermarking. Furthermore, the signal-to-masking ratio is further reduced indicating that in coding applications this approach can lead to further bit rate reduction without quality degradation.

Based on this psychoacoustic model, we presented in this chapter a high quality perceptual audio codec which employs a similar structure to MPEG 1 layer 3 (mp3) standard, including quantization and Huffman coding. The evaluation of this perceptual audio codec shows that the proposed audio codec achieves transparency coding and outperforms the mp3 codec by providing better audio quality with the same bit rates.

REFERENCES

He, X., & Scordilis, M. M.(2008-b), Psychoacoustic music analysis based on the discrete wavelet packet transform. *Research Letters in Signal Processing.* doi:10.1155/2008/346767

ISO/IEC, 11172-3 (1993). Coding of moving picture and associated audio for digital storage media at up to about 1.5 Mbits - part 3 audio.

Sinha, D., & Tewfik, A. (1993). Low bit rate transparent audio compression using adapted wavelets. *IEEE Transactions on Signal Processing, 41*(12), 3463–3479. doi:10.1109/78.258086

Chapter 10
A Novel Spread Spectrum Digital Audio Watermarking Scheme

This chapter proposes a novel spread spectrum technology with improved synchronization capacity. This enhanced spread spectrum technology together with the previously proposed psychoacoustic model are incorporated into a digital audio watermarking system, which shows better performance compared to systems introduced by other researchers.

10.1 INTRODUCTION

The increase in computational power and the proliferation of the Internet has facilitated the production and distribution of unauthorized copies of multimedia information. As a result, the problem of copyright protection has attracted the interest of the worldwide scientific and the business communities. The most promising

DOI: 10.4018/978-1-61520-925-5.ch010

solution seems to be the watermarking process where the original data is marked with ownership information hidden in an imperceptible manner in the original signal. Understanding of the human perception processes is the key to successful watermarking. Typical properties of a successful watermarking scheme includes (Cox et al., 2002)

a.   The watermark should introduce no perceptual distortion.
b.   The watermark should be embedded into the host signal, rather than into a header.
c.   The watermark should be hard to remove, or even detect without the prior knowledge of the watermarking scheme and the watermark sequence.
d.   The watermark should be self-clocking, which also know as synchronization problem.
e.   The watermark should be readily extracted to completely characterize the copyright owner.

Several techniques in audio watermarking system have been developed in the past decade including lowest-bit coding, phase coding, echo coding, spread spectrum (Bender et al., 1996). Compared to embedding watermark into still images, audio watermarking is much more challenging due to the extreme sensitivity of the human auditory system to changes in the audio signal (Cox et al., 2002). In order to make the embedded watermarks inaudible, a suitable psychoacoustic model is at most of the time, an indispensable part of a good audio watermarking scheme.

Many digital audio watermarking schemes have benefited from the perceptual entropy psychoacoustic model used in several MPEG coding and successfully embedded the watermarks without introducing perceptible distortion (He et al., 2004, 2005; Swanson et al., 1998; S. Jung, et. al., 2003; Garcia, 1999). For example, in (Swanson et al., 1998), the authors first calculate the masking threshold using the psychoacoustic model from MPEG I layer 1 and embed the watermarks to the frequency locations where the signal energy is below the threshold, thus avoiding audible distortion.

S. Jung, et al. (2003) embedded watermarks in the discrete cosine domain (DCT) with the psychoacoustic model from MPEG-2 advanced audio coding (AAC) encoding system. A spectral envelope filter was introduced in the detection phase to reduce the noise variance in the correlation, thus improving the detection bit error rate (BER).

Garcia (1999) proposed a digital audio watermarking scheme using a psychoacoustic model and spread spectrum theory. In this algorithm, the watermarks were locally repeated, interleaved, and spread. A psychoacoustic model was applied to the original audio and the masking thresholds of the audio signal were calculated in the frequency domain. The watermarks were spectrally shaped to fit under the masking threshold of the audio signal.

Seok et al. (2002) proposed an audio watermarking based on traditional direct sequence spread spectrum (DSSS) approach and achieved a watermark insertion rate of 8 bits per second (bps). The inaudibility of the watermark was maintained by incorporating the psychoacoustic model derived from the MPEG I layer I audio coding standard. Their experiments showed the audio watermarking system to be robust to several signal transformations and malicious attacks.

Most psychoacoustic models used in audio compression or watermarking, have so far utilized the short-time Fourier transform (STFT) to construct a time-varying spectral representation of the signal (Painter et al., 2000; Johnston, 1988; Bosi et al., 2003). A window sequence of fixed length is used to capture signal section, resulting in a fixed spectral resolution. However, the STFT can provide only averaged frequency information of the signal and it lacks the flexibility of arbitrary time-frequency localization (Polikar, online, 2006). Such a rigid analysis regime is in striking contrast with the unpredictably dynamic spectral-temporal profile of information-carrying audio signals. Instead, signal characteristics would be analyzed and represented more accurately by a more versatile description providing a time-frequency multi-resolution pertinent to the signal dynamics. The approaches included in MPEG 1 and elsewhere allow the switching between two different analysis window sizes depending on the value of the signal entropy (ISO/IEC, 1993), or the changes in the estimated signal variance (Lincoln, 1998). Greater flexibility, however, is needed. The wavelet transform presents an attractive alternative by providing frequency-dependent resolution, which can better match the hearing mechanism (Polikar, online). Specifically, long windows analyze low frequency components and achieve high frequency resolution while progressively shorter windows analyze higher frequency components to achieve better time resolution. Wavelet analysis has found numerous signal processing applications including video and image compression (Abbate et al., 2002; Jaffard et al., 2001), perceptual audio coding (Veldhuis et al., 1989), high quality audio compression and psychoacoustic model approximation (Sinha et al., 1993).

Wu et al. (2005) introduced an efficient self-synchronized audio watermarking for assured audio data transmission. The transparency of the watermarking was achieved by using a fixed watermarking strength factor instead of using the psychoacoustic model. However, as the authors commented, that the watermarking strength factor varied and experiments had to be conducted as new types of audio signals were encountered in order to specify its value. The need for such procedure greatly limits the application of this method.

Sinha et al. (1993) used the model for masking proposed by Veldhuis et al. (1989) to calculate the masking thresholds in frequency after computing the power spectrum using a fast Fourier transform. Those thresholds were used to find the constraint for the reconstruction error resulting from quantization or approximation of the wavelet coefficients. The constraints were then translated into the wavelet domain to ensure transparent wavelet audio coding.

Zurera et al. (2001) presented a new algorithm to translate psychoacoustic model information to the wavelet domain, even when low-selectivity filters were used to implement the wavelet transform or wavelet packet decomposition. They first calculated the masking thresholds in the frequency domain by Fourier transform. Based on several hypotheses, those thresholds sere divided by the equivalent filter frequency response magnitude of each filter bank branch forming the masking threshold in wavelet domain.

Reyes et al. (2003) further improved the psychoacoustic model in (Zurera et al., 2001) by introducing a new perceptual cost function which took into consideration both the wavelet representation of the input signal and the masking threshold estimated in the Fourier domain as well as the quantization noise power that can be inaudibly injected in the wavelet domain (Reyes et al., 2003).

Carnero et al. (1999) constructed a novel wavelet domain psychoacoustic model representation using a frame-synchronized fast wavelet packet transform algorithm. Frequency masking thresholds were estimated by steps similar to (Johnston, 1988). The energy in each sub band was calculated using wavelet coefficients, then the energy was shifted by the estimated tonality and spread by a spreading function. Temporal masking thresholds were found by further spreading the energy within each sub band. The final masking thresholds were obtained by considering those two thresholds as well as the absolute quiet thresholds per band.

In this chapter, an improved spread spectrum technique is used to embed watermarks into audio by taking advantages of the previously proposed psychoacoustic model, archiving better watermarking robustness as well as an enhanced synchronization / resynchronization algorithm.

It is widely acknowledged that the spread spectrum approach, although robust to common attacks, it is susceptible to synchronization attacks since the watermark has to be perfectly aligned with the stego-signal for possible recovery at the detection side. In our watermarking system we introduced an enhanced synchronization algorithm by using the time-frequency localization property of discrete wavelet packet transform (DWPT) from (Wu et al., 2005} as mentioned in Section 10.2.1.

An exhaustive search for the synchronization code is performed within a very limited space before any attempted recovery of watermarks. Since the searching space is now very small it enables fast exhaustive search for the synchronization code, thus reducing the computational cost and time delays in the watermarking system.

The chapter is organized as follows. In Section 10.2, we develop and present the improved watermarking system, including watermark design, insertion and detec-

Figure 1. Proposed watermarking system: encoder (top) and decoder (bottom)

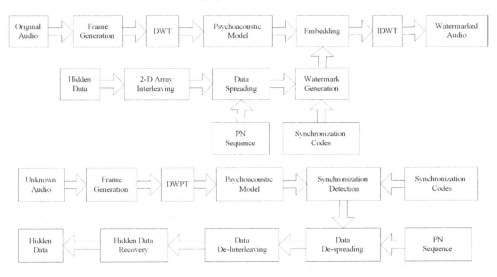

tion as well as an enhanced synchronization process by fast exhaustive searching in very limited reduced space. Section 10.3 shows the evaluation of the proposed watermarking system and compares its performance with previous work by other researchers. The last section is the conclusion.

10.2 WATERMARK DESIGN, INSERTION AND DETECTION

The proposed watermarking system encoding and decoding processes are summarized in Figure 1.

The encoder operates as follows (He, et al., 2006-b):

a.   The input original audio is segmented into overlapped frames of N samples long.
b.   Each frame is decomposed into 25 sub bands using the DWPT.
c.   The new psychoacoustic model is applied on those sub bands to determine the masking thresholds for each sub band.
d.   The data to be embedded (hidden data) is interleaved to enhance watermarking robustness.
e.   The interleaved data is spread by a PN sequence.
f.   Synchronization codes are attached at the beginning of the spread data, thus producing the final watermarks to be embedded.

g.   Watermark embedding into the original audio is conditional on the masking thresholds constraints.

h.   Inverse DWPT (IDWTP) is applied on the above data to obtain the watermarked audio back to the time domain.

The system decoder works in a reverse manner as the encoder as in Figure 1

a.   The incoming audio is first segmented into overlapped frames.

b.   The frame is decomposed into 25 sub bands by DWPT in wavelet domain.

c.   The same psychoacoustic model is applied on the data in wavelet domain determine the masking thresholds.

d.   Synchronization is performed by searching for the synchronization codes.

e.   The appropriate data are then de-spread, de-interleaved in order to detect and recover any hidden data.

10.2.1 The Synchronization Process

Similar to most spread spectrum-based watermarking systems encoder-decoder synchronization is achieved by attaching synchronization codes prior to watermark spreading during encoding. The synchronization code is typically a PN sequence which is able to withstand de-synchronization attacks, such as random cropping and shifting.

During decoding, the synchronization process has to be performed before the attempted recovery of the watermark. The necessary exhaustive search for the synchronization code in the watermarked stego-signal requires large amounts of processing power and memory usage and it introduces long system delays in the recovery process. These limitations prohibit an exhaustive synchronization search in many watermarking systems that require real-time processing.

In the proposed approach, a fast search in limited space is instead performed to detect the existence of the synchronization code. Fast search of synchronization is possible due to the time-frequency localization properties of the DWPT (Wu et al., 2005):

Suppose $\{a_j\}$ is the original audio, M is a frame within $\{a_j\}$, N is another frame shifted by 2^k samples from M, with the same length, $c_j^{k,M}$ and $c_j^{k,N}$ are the jth wavelet coefficients of M and N after the k-level DWPT decomposition, then

$$c_{j+1}^{k,M} = c_j^{k,N} \qquad (10.1)$$

Figure 2. Synchronization code detection

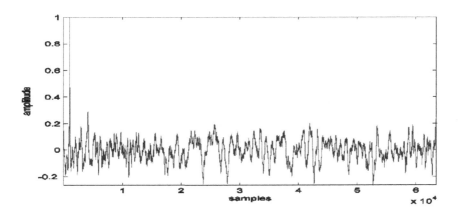

for all the coefficients in the frame except for less than $L+2$ coefficients where L is the length of the wavelet filter (Wu et al.,2005). Since the length of the frame is usually much longer than length of the wavelet filter (for example, in the proposed method, the frame length is 2048 while the length of wavelet filter is 16), those $L+2$ different coefficients have little effect on synchronization. In other words, in order to find one synchronization code within the watermarked audio, the decoder needs to perform at most $2^k (k = 8$ in our case) times sample by sample searches instead of D times sample by sample searches, where D is the length of the spread watermark. This approach provides substantial efficiency improvement in detection.

A typical search result is shown in Figure 2 where the peak indicates the starting position of the synchronization code. In this case, perfect synchronization between encoder and decoder watermark was achieved. However, attacks may damage watermarks and in that case detections peak are not pronounced, as shown in the example on Figure 3, where a watermark in another frame has been seriously damaged.

Since typically multiple watermark copies are inserted in various locations it is best to skip the seriously damaged watermarks and only decode information from watermarks with less or no damage. A watermark quality detector is implemented for this purpose as the "p_ratio", which is defined as

$$pratio = \frac{\max(o)}{\dfrac{\sum |o|}{N}} \qquad (10.2)$$

Figure 3. Damaged synchronization code

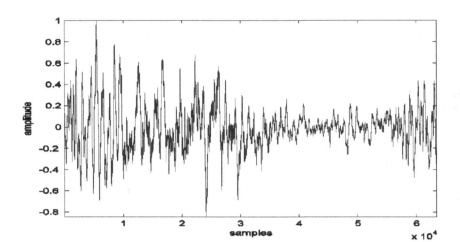

where o is the output of the detection filter and N is the length of o. Only when *p_ratio > threshold*, the watermarked audio frame is considered as not seriously damaged and watermark recovery is performed on this frame. A majority rule is used to recover the final watermark, as described in Section 10.2.4. By eliminate seriously damaged watermarks using Equation 10.2 detections becomes robust even when the signal undergoes severe attacks and compression as described in Section 10.4.

10.2.2 2-D Array Interleaving and Watermark Generation

The watermark is first repeated for M times (Kirovski et al., 2003) and then inter-leaved by a 2-D array (Garcia, 1999). The purpose of the 2-D array interleaving is to enhance the robustness for additive noise.

Suppose the data to be embedded has N samples denoted by $\{m_i\}$ consists of '1's and '-1's ('0's in the watermark are transformed into '-1' to enhance the robustness), first every sample in $\{m_i\}$ is locally repeated M times and we have the sequence:

$$\{m_1 m_1 m_1 ... m_2 m_2 m_2 ... m_N m_N ... m_N\}$$

The new data sequence is interleaved by a 2-D array with the size N*M (N rows by M columns), the above sequence is written to the array row by row and read out column by column to form a new data sequence as

Table 1. Data interleaving example

1	1	1	1	1
-1	-1	-1	-1	-1
-1	-1	-1	-1	-1
1	1	1	1	1

$$\{m_1 m_2 ... m_N m_1 m_2 ... m_N ... m_1 m_2 ... m_N\}$$

The purpose of interleaving is to enhance the robustness of the watermark for additive noise, especially the pulse like noise.

Suppose more than M/2 samples of the same symbol in the un-interleaved watermark are corrupted by the noise during transmission or attack, then that symbol can not be recovered at the decoder end. If the watermark is interleaved before embedding, there will be a better chance to recover it later.

An example is given below to illustrate the interleave idea.

Suppose the data to be embed is a '1001' and since '0's are transformed into '-1's, so the data become '1 -1 -1 1'. Then the each symbol repeats M times (M equals to 5 in this example) and the sequence now is '1 1 1 1 1 -1 -1 -1 -1 -1 -1 -1 -1 -1 -1 1 1 1 1 1'. The repeated data is written into a 5*4 2-D array by rows and we have the Table 1.

The data is now read out column by column into a sequence before embedding so we have the new sequence as:

'1 -1 -1 1 1 -1 -1 1 1 -1 -1 1 1 -1 -1 1 1 -1 -1 1'.

If during transmission, the first 8 symbols are corrupted, and the decoder receives the sequence 'x x x x x x x x 1 1 -1 -1 1 1 -1 -1 1 1 -1 -1 1' where 'x' denotes unknown symbol ('1' or '-1').

De-interleaving is performed on the sequence by writing it into the same 2-D array by column and we have Table 2.

The data in the de-interleaving array are read out row by row and we have 'x x 1 1 1 x x -1 -1 -1 x x -1 -1 -1 x x 1 1 1'.

The decision rule for the kth symbol of the recovered watermark is

$$w_k = \begin{cases} 1 & if \ r_k > 0 \\ -1 & if \ r_k \leq 0 \end{cases} \qquad (10.3)$$

Table 2. Data de-interleaving example

X	X	1	1	1
X	X	-1	-1	-1
X	X	-1	-1	-1
X	X	1	1	1

where

$$r_k = \sum_{i=(k-1)*M+1}^{k*M} m_i \qquad (10.4)$$

M is the repetition number (M is 5 in this example), m_i is the ith symbol in the above sequence.

According to the decision rule:

$$r_1 = r_4 = x + x + 1 + 1 + 1 = 3 + 2 * x > 0$$

$$r_2 = r_3 = x + x - 1 - 1 - 1 = -3 + 2 * x < 0$$

so $w_1=w_4=1$ and $w_2=w_3=-1$ and the recovered watermark is: '1 -1 -1 1' the same as the embedded one.

By interleaving the embedded watermark, the possible noise is averaged by the number of rows.

On the other hand, if no interleave is involved during the embedding process, the sequence that the decoder received will be 'x x x x x x x x -1 -1 -1 -1 -1 -1 -1 1 1 1 1 1'. We can easily see that the decoder can only recover the last two symbols correctly while the first two symbols are lost.

More detailed information about the interleave / de-interleave could be found in (Garcia, 1999).

10.2.3 Watermark Generation and Embedding

In order to enhance the robustness against additive noise corruption, signal compression and other attacks the watermark is first repeated M times (Kirovski et al., 2003) and then interleaved by an array similar to (Garcia, 1999). The modified watermark is then embedded in all spectral components below the masking thresholds, including the perceptually significant components of the audio signal, which are typically located in the low frequency area.

A threshold is used to measure the output of the matched filter at the decoder and we only try to recover less damaged watermarks, preventing the introduction of errors that would result from considering severely damaged watermarks as well.

The embedding process involves calculating the masking thresholds and spreading the watermark with PN sequence. Suppose that the data to be embedded are $\{m_k\}$, which are normalized wavelet coefficients of the watermark within the range of -1 and 1, for each frame. The embedding rule is:

$$c_k = \begin{cases} c_k + \alpha * m_i & if c_k^2 > T \\ \sqrt{T} * m_i & if c_k^2 \leq T \end{cases} \tag{10.5}$$

where c_k is the value of the *k-th* wavelet coefficient in the frame, α is a factor $(0 \leq \alpha \leq 1)$ used to control the watermark strength, m_i is the symbol to be embedded in this frame and T is the masking threshold for that frequency sub band. Increasing α typically improves watermarking system robustness by embedding higher energy watermark. However this occurs at the risk of introducing perceptual distortion. In our system, α is set to 0 to ensure transparent watermarking.

10.2.4 Watermark Extraction

In the decoding phase, the input signal is first segmented into overlapping frames and the masking thresholds for the sub band in each frame are calculated.

Let $d = \sum c_k$, where c_k is the *k-th* wavelet coefficient in the frame and satisfies $c_k^2 \leq T$, where T is the masking threshold for that frequency sub band. Then the recovery decision rule is

$$w = \begin{cases} 1 & if d > 0 \\ -1 & if d \leq 0 \end{cases} \tag{10.6}$$

The data w is then de-spread by the same PN sequence, de-interleaved by the same array and output a sequence $\{m_i\}$. The *kth* symbol of the watermark is recovered using the following decision rule

$$W_k = \begin{cases} 1 & if r_k > 0 \\ -1 & if r_k \leq 0 \end{cases} \tag{10.7}$$

where

$$r_k = \sum_{i=(k-1)\times M+1}^{k\times M} m_i \tag{10.8}$$

M is the repetition number, m_i is the *ith* symbol in the above-mentioned sequence $\{m_i\}$.

Suppose N watermarks are recovered individually and the length of each watermark is D, then the *k-th* symbol of the final recovered watermark is

$$W_k = sign(\sum_{i=1}^{N} w_{i,k}) \tag{10.9}$$

where $w_{i,k}$ is the *k-th* symbol of the *i-th* recovered watermark ($1 \leq k \leq D$) and *sign* is the function defined as:

$$sign(k) = \begin{cases} 1 & if k > 0 \\ -1 & if k \leq 0 \end{cases} \tag{10.10}$$

By using the majority rule, we can recover the final watermark even when individual watermarks are not error free.

10.3 EXPERIMENTAL PROCEDURES AND RESULTS

In this section, experiments are conducted to validate the advantages reached by integrating the proposed psychoacoustic model into the watermarking system.

10.3.1 System Robustness Test

The same audio material was used to test the robustness of the proposed watermarking scheme. The test watermark is consisted of 168 bits of information and the embedding process achieved a watermark bit rate of 8.4 bps. The 168bits watermark is embedded into 131072 audio samples, considering the 50% overlap while each 2048 samples long frame contains an average of 1.32 watermark bits

Several attacks are carried out against the proposed watermarking system and the results are shown in Table 3. These attacks are:

a. *Random cropping:* 20000 samples are randomly deleted from or added to the watermarked audio in 10 different locations.
b. *Re-sampling:* The watermarked CD quality audio is down sampled to 22.05 kHz and then up sampled to 44.1 kHz.
c. *DA / AD conversion:* The watermarked CD quality audio is played out and the output is recorded back through the line-in jack on the sound card of the same computer and sampled at 44.1 kHz.
d. *Amplitude compression:* The audio signal amplitude is compressed with a non-linear gain function that changes with time.
e. *Echo addition:* The audio signal is filtered with $h(t) = \delta(t) + 0.5\delta(t - 0.1)$ to add a 100 ms echo.
f. *Equalization*: The original audio signal is distorted by a 10-band equalizer which has 6 dB gain in the 62 Hz, 250 Hz, 1000 Hz, 4000 Hz and 16000 Hz bands and -6 dB gain in the 31 Hz, 125 Hz, 500 Hz, 2000 Hz and 8000 Hz bands.

Table 3. Proposed watermarking system bit error rate after attacks

Attack\Audio	Country BER (%)	Jazz BER (%)	Pop BER (%)	Rock BER (%)	Classic BER (%)	AVERAGE BER (%)
AWGNSNR=20dB	0	0	0	0	0	0
AWGN SNR=10dB	2.98	2.33	1.38	0.25	3.25	2.04
AWGN SNR=5dB	8.15	7.19	3.75	2.97	7.66	5.94
CNA	0.52	0	0	0	0.06	0.12
LP Filtering	0.08	0	0.79	1.68	0.12	0.53
HP Filtering	0	0	0.27	0.25	0	0.10
BP Filtering	0.79	1.71	2.03	0.36	1.76	1.33
MP3 @ 64 kbps	0.79	0.79	0.52	0.25	0.19	0.50
MP3 @ 32 kbps	2.03	1.61	3.33	0.36	1.44	1.75

g. *White Gaussian noise addition:* White Gaussian noise was added to the watermarked audio for an average SNR of 20 dB, 10dB and 5dB.

h. *Color noise addition:* WGN is filtered by the estimated masking threshold to simulate just audible colored noise that changes on a frame-by-frame basis and then added to each signal frame to interfere with the embedded watermark

i. *Filtering:* The watermarked audio undergoes different filtering process. In the test three filters are used and they are lowpass filter (passband frequency = 5000 Hz, stopband frequency = 6000 Hz), highpass filter (stopband frequency = 1000 Hz, passband frequency = 2000 Hz) and bandpass filter (first stopband frequency = 50 Hz, first passband frequency = 1000 Hz, second passband frequency = 5000 Hz, second stopband frequency = 6000 Hz). The stopband attenuation factor is set to 0.0001 for all the filters.

j. *MPEG compression:* The watermarked audio is compressed into an MP3 format at various bit rates and then decompressed back into a wave file.

Table 3 summarizes the results obtained by watermarking the test audio material, subjecting to the described attacks and measuring the distortion in the extracted watermark as percentage bit error rate (% BER) and averaged for the entire test signal set. Watermarks are recovered perfectly (BER=0) in first six attack scenarios ranging from random cropping to equalization. For the rest situations, some errors are detected, for instance in the case of MP3 compression, but the performance is still very good with average BER of down to 1.75% for the extremely low 32 kbps compression rate. Even in such cases perfect watermark recovery is often achieved because in the proposed system the final recovered watermark results from a majority rule applied on multiple inserted watermarks.

Subjective listening tests were conducted confirming that by embedding the watermark with the proposed technique the processed audio signals are indistinguishable from the original resulting in an audibly transparent process

10.3.2 Watermarking Systems Comparison

In this section, we compare the proposed system to the watermarking system based on the traditional PE based psychoacoustic model. Watermark generation for the PE watermarking system was based on the use of direct sequence spread spectrum (DSSS), similar to that proposed by Seok et al. (2002}. Both systems carried watermark payload of 8 bps and used the entire music material available for testing, as described earlier. The watermark audio obtained from both techniques underwent the same attacks, as in Section 5.3.1. The PE watermarking system achieves perfect recovery after it undergoes the more simple attacks that included random cropping, re-sampling, amplitude compression, echo addition and equalization. However, errors occurred as a result of noise addition, DA/AD conversion and MPEG compression, and the effects of those attacks were further studied for both system.

Three key parameters are critical in the evaluation of a watermarking scheme: robustness, watermark payload and watermark length. Watermark should be robust for copyright protection purposes, which is reason for the existence of most current watermarking systems. Watermark payload should be high enough to provide room for embedding reasonable amounts of metadata or copyright information. The watermark length should be long enough to minimize detection errors but and be short enough to reduce the processing delay and computational complexity at the detector (Kirovski et al., 2003). Furthermore, short watermarks also reduce the risk of detecting the watermark locations by adversaries. In general, good watermark robustness, high watermark payload and short watermark length are desired by almost all watermarking systems in any application.

Since the proposed psychoacoustic model provides more room for watermark embedding and greater reduction of the SSMR, we expect the proposed watermarking system to provide a better watermark robustness, higher watermark payload and shorter watermark length compared to the PE model based watermarking system. A series of comparison experiments were performed in order to validate this assertion and are described in the sequel. The obtained results were averaged for both watermarking systems and were obtained using the entire audio test material.

10.3.3 Watermark Robustness Comparison

In this experiment, we compare the proposed system to PE model system with the results obtained in Section 10.3.1 and 10.3.2.

Both watermarking systems have the same watermark payload of 8.4 bps and the same watermark length of 131072 samples, which spans 2.9722 seconds in the tested music files at 44.1 kHz sampling rate.

The robustness results are listed in Table 4.

Table 4 shows that with the same watermark payload and watermark length the proposed watermarking scheme is more robust and survives better in noise addition, DA/AD conversion and MP3 compression attacks than the PE method.

10.3.4 Watermark Payload Comparison

In this experiment, we attempted to insert more useful information in the watermarks in the proposed system while maintaining the same watermark length for both approaches.

The PE model system remains the same as in Section 5.3.3 with 8.4 bps watermark payload and 131072 samples long watermark length. On the other hand, the

Table 4. Watermark robustness comparison with PE method

Attack Type	PE Method BER (%)	Proposed Method BER (%)
Noise Addition	3.0	0
DA/AD Conversion	1.5	0
MP3 64 kbps Compression	3.5	0.5

proposed watermarking system employs the same length of watermark, embeds 208 bits information into each audio clip, achieving 10.4 bps watermark payload, which is 24% higher than the PE model system.

The obtained robustness results are depicted in Table 5.

From Table 5, we can clearly see that although the proposed system obtained a much higher watermark payload, it still demonstrates similar robustness compared to the PE model.

10.3.5 Watermark Length Comparison

During this experiment, we try to achieve in the proposed watermarking system the same watermark robustness with the same watermark payload but a shorter length watermark compared to the PE model system.

The PE model system is the same as in Section 10.3.3, which has 8bps watermark payload with 131072 samples long watermark length, the proposed system, on the other hand, realizes 8.4 bps watermark payload with a 65536 samples long watermark, which is only the half length of the one incorporated in the PE model. The robustness results are shown in Table 6.

From Table 6, we can easily see that the proposed watermark system provides similar watermark robustness to the PE model with the same watermark payload, but 50% shorter watermark.

Table 5. Watermark payload comparison with PE method

Attack Type	PE Method BER (%) (at 8.4 bps)	Proposed Method BER (%) (at 10.4 bps)
Noise Addition	3.0	1.6
DA/AD Conversion	1.5	1.5
MP3 64 kbps Compression	3.5	3.4

Table 6. Watermark length comparison with PE method

Attack Type	PE Method BER (%) (131072 samples)	Proposed Method BER (%) (65536 samples)
Noise Addition	3.0	1.9
DA/AD Conversion	1.5	1.5
MP3 64 kbps Compression	3.5	3.1

10.4 CONCLUSION

In this chapter, we have presented an audio watermarking scheme with an improved spread spectrum method and an enhanced psychoacoustic model using wavelet packet transform (DWPT). The psychoacoustic model introduced in the watermarking system accurately calculates the masking and auditory thresholds in the wavelet domain by closely approximating the critical bands, which makes the watermarking process transparent.

As mentioned in chapter 7, the proposed method also provides broader masking capabilities compared to the DFT based psychoacoustic model proposed in (Johnston, 1988), thus revealing that larger signal regions are in fact inaudible and therefore providing more space for watermark embedding without noticeable effect. Furthermore, the signal-to-masking ratio is further reduced indicating that in audio watermarking applications this approach can lead to further watermark robustness by embedding relative higher energy watermarks without quality degradation.

The improved spread spectrum technique employs an advanced synchronization method, which makes it possible for the system to resynchronize after the possible attacks. As it is widely reported in the literature, the synchronization problem is, most of the time, the weakest link in spread spectrum based digital audio watermarking scheme.

Extensive experiments show this method is robust to many attacks, while in those case where errors do occur the performance is respectable. Because the watermarks are repeated many times in the host audio, those errors are usually removed by applying a majority rule on the data of the recovered watermark copies. When compared to the standard perceptual entropy psychoacoustic model-based spread spectrum watermarking system, the proposed watermarking system provides improved system performance by offering better watermark robustness, higher watermark payload and shorter watermark length.

REFERENCES

Abbate, A., Decusatis, C. M., & Das, P. K. (2002). *Wavelets and subbands, fundamentals and applications*. Boston, MA: Birkhauser.

Bender, W., Gruhl, D., Morimoto, N., & Lu, A. (1996). Techniques for data hiding. *IBM Systems Journal, 35*(3/4), 313–336. doi:10.1147/sj.353.0313

Bosi, M., & Goldberg, R. E. (2003). *Introduction to digital audio coding and standards*. Norwell, MA: Kluwer Academic Publishers.

Carnero, B., & Drygajlo, A. (1999). Perceptual speech coding and enhancement using frame-synchronized fast wavelet packet transform algorithms. *IEEE Transactions on Signal Processing, 47*(6), 1622–1635. doi:10.1109/78.765133

Cox, I. J., Miller, M. L., & Bloom, J. A. (2002). *Digital watermarking*. San Francisco, CA: Academic Press.

Garcia, R. A. (1999). Digital watermarking of audio signals using a psychoacoustic model and spread spectrum theory. In *Proceedings of the 107th Convention of Audio Engineering Society (AES)* (Preprint 5073). New York, NY.

He, X., Iliev, A., & Scordilis, M. M. (2004). A novel high capacity digital audio watermarking system. In *Proceedings of the IEEE International Conference on Acoustics, Speech and Signal Processing (ICASSP)*,(pp. 393-396).

He, X., & Scordilis, M. M. (2005). Improved spread spectrum digital audio Watermarking Based on Modified Perceptual Entropy Psychoacoustic Model. In *Proceedings of the IEEE Southeast Conference* (pp. 283-286). Miami, FL.

He, X., & Scordilis, M. M. (2006b). *An Improved spread spectrum digital audio watermarking scheme based on a psychoacoustic model using wavelet packet transform algorithms*. IEEE Transactions on Information Forensics and Security.

ISO/IEC, 11172-3 (1993). Coding of moving picture and associated audio for digital storage media at up to about 1.5 Mbits - part 3 audio.

Jaffard, S., Meyer, Y., & Ryan, R. D. (2001). *Wavelets tools for science and technology*. Philadelphia, PA: SIAM.

Johnston, J. D. (1998). Transform coding of audio signals using perceptual noise criteria. *IEEE Journal on Selected Areas in Communications, 6*(2), 314–323. doi:10.1109/49.608

Jung, S., Seok, J., & Hong, J. (2003). An improved detection technique for spread spectrum audio watermarking with a spectral envelope filter. *ETRI, 25*(1), 52–54. doi:10.4218/etrij.03.0203.0103

Kirovski, D., & Malvar, H. S. (2003). Spread-spectrum watermarking of audio signals. *IEEE Transactions on Signal Processing, 51*(4), 1020–1033. doi:10.1109/TSP.2003.809384

Lincoln, B. (1998). An experimental high fidelity perceptual audio coder. *Project in MUS420* Retrieved from http://www-ccrma.stanford.edu/ jos/bosse/.

Painter, T., & Spanias, A. (2000). Perceptual coding of digital audio. *Proceedings of the IEEE, 88*(4), 451–513. doi:10.1109/5.842996

Polikarg, R. (2006). The wavelet tutorial. Retrieved from http://users.rowan.edu/polikar/Wavelets/wtpart1.html

Reyes, N. R., Zurera, M. R., Ferreras, F. L., & Amores, P. J. (2003). Adaptive wavelet-packet analysis for audio coding purposes. *Signal Processing, 83,* 919–929. doi:10.1016/S0165-1684(02)00489-9

Seok, J., Hong, J., & Kim, J. (2002). A novel audio watermarking algorithm for copyright protection of digital audio. *ETRI Journal, 24*(3), 181–189. doi:10.4218/etrij.02.0102.0301

Sinha, D., & Tewfik, A. (1993). Low bit rate transparent audio compression using adapted wavelets. *IEEE Transactions on Signal Processing, 41*(12), 3463–3479. doi:10.1109/78.258086

Swanson, M. D., Zhu, B., Tewfik, A. H., & Boney, L. (1998). Robust audio watermarking using perceptual masking. *Elsevier Signal Processing, Special Issue on Copyright Protection and Access Control, 66*(3), 337–355.

Veldhuis, R. N. J., Breeuwer, M., & Van Der Wall, R. G. (1989). Subband coding of digital audio signals. *Philips Journal of Research, 44*(2/3), 329–343.

Wu, S., Huang, J., Huang, D., & Shi, Y. Q. (2005). Efficiently self-synchronized audio watermarking for assured audio data transmission. *IEEE Transactions on Broadcasting, 51*(1), 69–76. doi:10.1109/TBC.2004.838265

Zurera, M. R., Ferreras, F. L., Amores, M. P. J., Bascon, S. M., & Reyes, N. R. (2001). A new algorithm for translating psychoacoustic information to the wavelet domain. *Signal Processing, 81,* 519–531. doi:10.1016/S0165-1684(00)00230-9

Chapter 11
Further Improvements of the Watermarking Scheme

In the previous chapter, we have proposed a watermarking scheme that embeds watermarks into the host signal where the audio power spectrum is below the masking threshold. This scheme, although proven to be better than the PE psychoacoustic model based watermarking scheme, still has room for further improvements. In this section, we will propose an enhanced watermarking scheme that not only embeds the watermark into the below masking threshold area, but also takes advantage the HAS properties and inserts the watermark into the audible spectrum areas and still keep the introduced distortion imperceptible.

DOI: 10.4018/978-1-61520-925-5.ch011

Figure 1. New proposed watermarking system: encoder (top) and decoder (bottom)

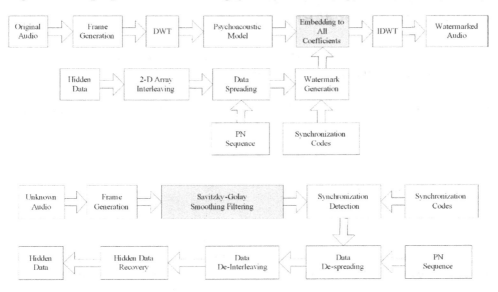

11.1 DIAGRAM OF PROPOSED ENHANCED WATERMARK SYSTEM

The diagram of the enhanced watermarking system (encoder and decoder) is illustrated in Figure 1.

Comparing Figure 1 in the current chapter with Figure 1 in chapter 10, we can see that the differences between the enhanced system and the previously proposed one are:

a. For the enhanced encoder, the watermarks are embedded into all wavelet coefficients, regardless of the host signal wavelet power spectrum distribution. In the previously proposed encoder, however, the watermarks are only embedded to the area where the host signal wavelet power spectrum is below the masking thresholds.

b. For the enhanced decoder, the psychoacoustic model is dropped off and replaced by a Savitzky-Golay smoothing filter (William et al., 1992), which is used to de-correlate the host signal and the watermark and decrease the interference from the host signal. Since no psychoacoustic model is needed, the enhanced decoder performs much faster than the previously introduced due to the huge amount saved from the reduction of the masking thresholds estimation.

11.2 ENCODER OF THE PROPOSED ENHANCED WATERMARK SYSTEM

The procedure of the enhanced embedding is similar to the previously proposed, which involves calculating the masking thresholds and spreading the watermark with a PN sequence. Suppose that the data to be embedded are $\{m_k\}$, which are normalized wavelet coefficients of the watermark within the range of -1 and 1, for each frame. The embedding rule is:

$$c_k = \begin{cases} c_k + \alpha * m_i & if c_k^2 > T \\ \sqrt{T} * m_i & if c_k^2 \leq T \end{cases} \tag{11.1}$$

where c_k is the value of the *k-th* wavelet coefficient in the frame, α is a factor ($0 \leq \alpha \leq 1$) used to control the watermark strength, m_i is the symbol to be embedded in this frame and T is the masking threshold for that frequency sub band. Increasing α typically improves watermarking system robustness by embedding higher energy watermarks. Unlike before, however, α is set in a way that watermarks could be embedded into those above masking thresholds areas without introducing perceptual distortion into the host audio signal.

According to (Swanson et. al., 1998), the introduced distortion is imperceptible as long as its energy is kept below the masking threshold. In our system, we set

$$\alpha = 0.95\sqrt{T} \tag{11.2}$$

in order to assure transparent watermark embedding.

Figure 2 to Figure 5 list a typical one frame of audio power spectrum, watermark power spectrum, watermark power spectrum after noise shaping, watermarked audio power spectrum and the masking thresholds.

As we can see from Figure 3 and Figure 4, the watermarked power spectrum is shaped due to psychoacoustic model constraints and falls below the masking thresholds. In Figure 5, the watermarked audio power spectrum is elevated in certain regions compared to the original audio. However, since the embedded watermark power spectrum is below the masking threshold, the distortion introduced into the watermarked audio remains imperceptible, which is confirmed by our listening test.

Figure 2. Typical one frame audio power spectrum

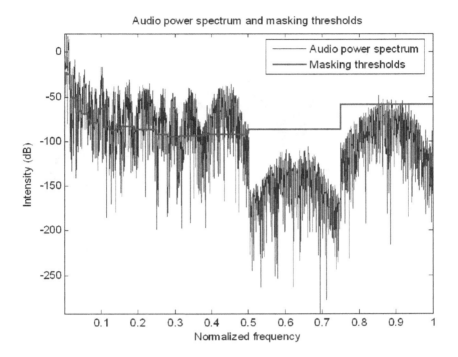

11.3 DECODER OF PROPOSED ENHANCED WATERMARK SYSTEM

In the decoder side, the enhanced system drops off the complex and time consuming psychoacoustic model computation. The input audio is divided into frames and each frame is pre-processed by a Savitzky-Golay smoothing filter to reduce the interference from the host signal.

A matched filter is used to detect the location of the watermark by tracking the synchronization code, which is a modulated PN sequence. The matched filter detection is optimal in the sense of SNR in the additive white Gaussian channel. However, the host audio signal is generally far from being additive white Gaussian noise as adjacent audio samples are highly correlated, which leads to the optimal detection problem using a pre-processing of audio with de-correlation of audio samples before detection. Therefore, the presumption for an optimal signal detection in the sense of signal to noise ratio is not satisfied, especially if extraction calculations are performed in short time windows of audio signal.

137

Figure 3. Typical one frame watermark power spectrum

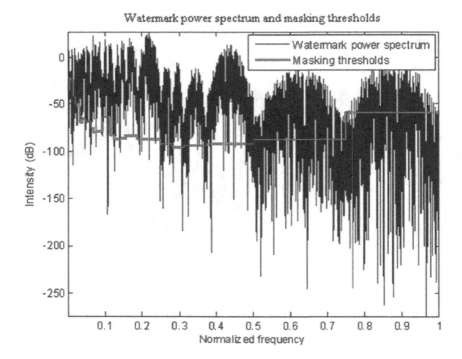

In order to decrease correlation between the samples of the audio signal, the decoder incorporates the least squares Savitzky-Golay smoothing filters (with different polynomial order and window length), which are typically used to "smooth out" a noise signal whose frequency span is large (Cvejic, 2004).

Rather than having their properties defined in the Fourier domain, and then translated to the time domain, Savitzky-Golay filters derive directly from a particular formulation of the data-smoothing problem in the time domain. The Savitzky-Golay filters are optimal in the sense that they minimize the least square errors in fitting a polynomial to frames of noisy data. Equivalently, the idea is to approximate the underlying function within a moving window by a polynomial.

Suppose the watermarked signal is x and the residual signal is r, then

$$r = x - sg(x) \tag{11.3}$$

Figure 4. Typical one frame watermark power spectrum after shaping

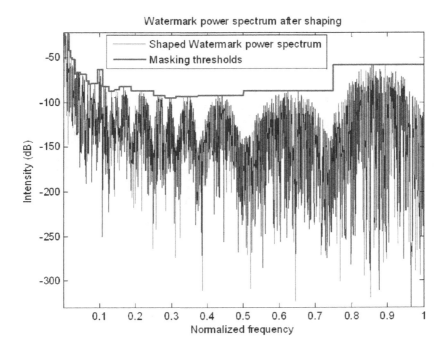

where sg(x) is the smoothed version of watermarked audio x obtained by pre-processing of Savitzky-Golay smoothing filtering.

Figure 6 shows the typical watermarked audio, its smoothed version and the residual signal. As we can see the residual signal is more noise like, which contains most of the watermark information.

Figure 7 and Figure 8 show the output of the matched filter applying on the same frame of watermarked audio, one without Savitzky-Golay smooth filter pre-processing and one with the pre-processing, respectively. As we can clearly see from those figures, the output in Figure 8 is more white noise-like and the peak is much easier to detect than in Figure 7. Watermark information is preserved much better in Figure 8 than in Figure 7, which is proven by our experimental results.

Figure 5. Typical one frame watermarked audio power spectrum

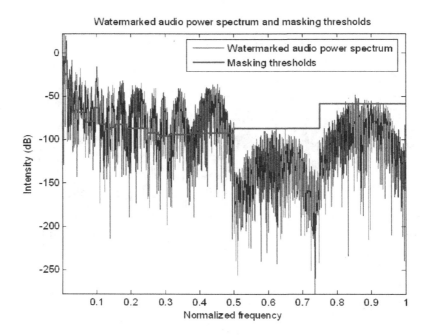

11.4 DISCUSSION ABOUT THE SAVITZKY-GOLAY SMOOTHING FILTER

In this section, we discussed in detail the Savitzky-Golay smoothing filter which we incorporated in previous section as pre-processing procedure to remove / minimize the interference from the host signal when decoding the watermarks.

Consider a normal digital filter with the following equation (William et al., 1992)

$$g_i = \sum_{n=-n_L}^{n_R} c_n f_{i+n} \tag{11.4}$$

where f_i is the input data, g_i is the output data and c_n is the filter coefficient, nL is the number of points used "to the left" of a data point i, i.e., earlier than it, while nR is the number used to the right, i.e., later. A so-called *causal* filter would have $nR = 0$.

The idea of Savitzky-Golay filtering is to find filter coefficients c_n that preserve higher moments, thus reducing the distortion of essential features of the data like peak heights and line widths in a spectrum, while the efficiency of the suppression

Figure 6. Typical watermarked audio signal pre-processing with Savitzky-Golay smoothing filter

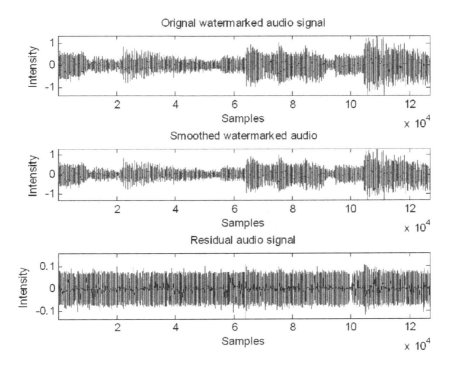

of random noise is effectively unchanged. In our case, the smoothed version of the watermarked audio will remains most of the features of the original host audio without much of the random noise, which is the watermark signal in this situation. On the other hand, the residual signal, which is the difference between the watermarked signal and the smoothed version of the watermarked signal, contains most of the watermark information.

Equivalently, the idea behind Savitzky-Golay filter is to approximate the underlying function within the moving window not by a constant (whose estimate is the average), but by a polynomial of higher order, typically quadratic or quartic: For each point f_i, we least-squares fit a polynomial to all nL + nR +1 points in the moving window, and then set g_i to be the value of that polynomial at position i. We make no use of the value of the polynomial at any other point. When we move on to the next point fi+1, we do a whole new least-squares fit using a shifted window.

To derive such c_n coefficients, consider how g_0 might be obtained: We want to fit a polynomial of degree M in i, namely $a_0 + a_1 i + \ldots + a_M i^M$ to the values $f-nL, \ldots, fnR$.

Figure 7. Typical output of the matched filter without Savitzky-Golay smoothing filter pre-processing

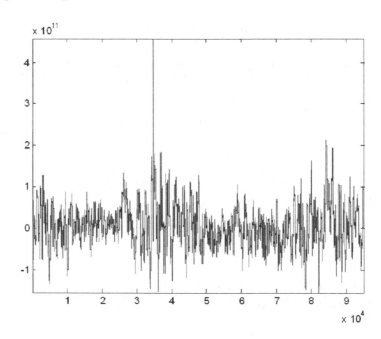

Then g_0 will be the value of that polynomial at $i = 0$, namely a_0. The design matrix for this problem is

$$A_{ij} = i^j$$
$$i = -nL, \ldots, nR, \; j = 0, \ldots, M$$

(11.5)

and the normal equations for the vector of *aj* 's in terms of the vector of *fi*'s is in matrix notation

$$(A^T \cdot A) \cdot a = A^T \cdot f \; or \; a = (A^T \cdot A)^{-1} \cdot (A^T \cdot f)$$

(11.6)

We also have the specific forms

$$\{A^T \cdot A\}_{ij} = \sum_{k=-n_L}^{n_R} A_{ki} A_{kj} = \sum_{k=-n_L}^{n_R} k^{i+j}$$

(11.7)

Figure 8. Typical output of the matched filter with Savitzky-Golay smoothing filter pre-processing

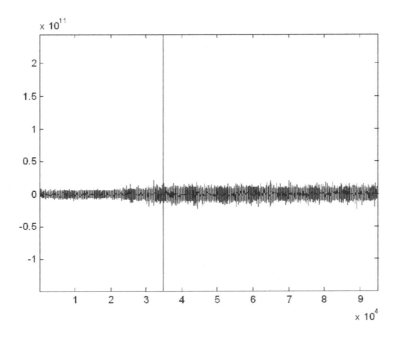

and

$$\{A^T \cdot f\}_j = \sum_{k=-n_L}^{n_R} A_{kj} f_k = \sum_{k=-n_L}^{n_R} k^j f_k \tag{11.8}$$

Since the coefficient c_n is the component $a0$ when **f** is replaced by the unit vector **e**n, $-nL \leq n < nR$, we have

$$c_n =$$
$$\{(A^T \cdot A)^{-1} \cdot (A \cdot e_n)\}_0 = \sum_{m=0}^{M} \{(A^T \cdot A)^{-1}\}_{0m} n^m \tag{11.9}$$

Since audio signal may have fast varying spectra, we set the moving window size as 6 samples long, which spans 0.13 seconds for 44.1 kHz sampling rate audio

Figure 9. Savitzky-Golay smoothing filter used in the system, impulse response, frequency response and phase response

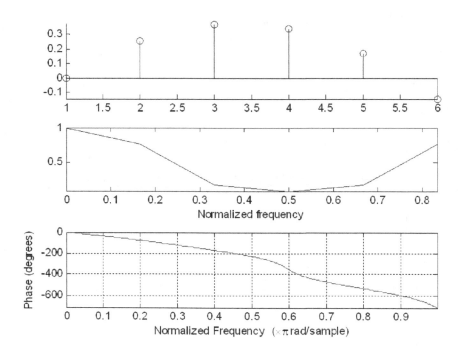

and adapts fast enough for all types of audio signals. We empirically set nL = 2, nR=3 and M=2 according to numerous experiments.

The impulse response, frequency response and phase response of the incorporated Savitzky-Golay smoothing filter are illustrated in Figure 9. As we can see from the figure, this Savitzky-Golay smoothing filter is a FIR filter with nearly linear phase response.

Figure 10 and Figure 11 illustrated the Savitzky-Golay smooth filter applied on one audio frame, as we will show in Chapter 12. Figure 10 shows the watermarked audio frame, its smoothed version and the residual signal in time domain. Figure 11 shows the same signals in frequency domain. Figure 12 shows the spectrum phase of the same signal and we can see that the residual signal has almost a linear phase spectrum.

The effects of Savitzky-Golay smooth filter has previously demonstrated in Figure 7 and Figure 8 where we can see that after pre-processing, the spike of the output from the matched filter is far more clear than the one without such pre-

Figure 10. Illustration of Savitzky-Golay smoothing filter on one frame, watermarked audio, smoothed audio and the residual audio in time domain

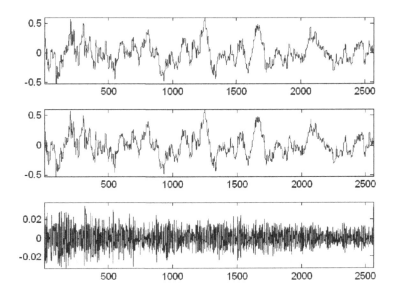

processing, which indicates a possible better watermark recovery, as proved by the experimental results in the next section.

11.5 EVALUATION OF THE PROPOSED ENHANCED WATERMARK SYSTEM

The same audio material was used to test the robustness of the proposed watermarking scheme. The test watermark is consisted of 168 bits of information and the embedding process achieved a watermark bit rate of 8.4 bps. The 168bits watermark is embedded into 131072 audio samples, considering the 50% overlap while each 2048 samples long frame contains an average of 1.32 watermark bits

Several attacks are carried out against the proposed watermarking system and the results are shown in Table 1.

The new watermarking system shows high robustness against many attacks. Watermarks are recovered perfectly (BER=0) in first six attack scenarios ranging from random cropping to equalization, which is the same as the proposed system

Figure 11. Illustration of Savitzky-Golay smoothing filter on one frame, watermarked audio, smoothed audio and residual audio in frequency domain

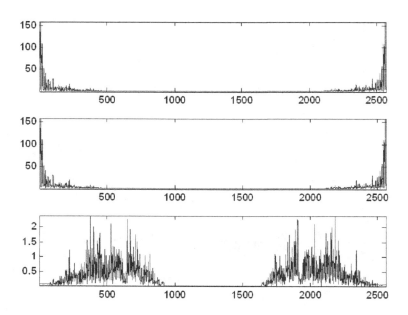

in previous chapter. However, the new system can recover watermarks perfectly from four more attacks i.e. white noise addition with SMR = 20 dB, 10 dB 5 dB as well as color noise addition. The new system also performs better filtering and MP3 compression test.

The benefits of the enhanced watermark system are:

a. *Robust against many signal processing or malicious attacks.* The improved system performs better in almost all the attacks compared to the previous one.
b. *Fast decoding process.* Since the time consuming psychoacoustic model calculation is dropped off and replaced by a Savitzky-Golay smooth filter, the decoding process is much faster than previously
c. *More secure.* This is perhaps the most important benefit we can get from the new watermarking system. In the previously proposed system, watermarks are embedded to the inaudible areas where the audio power spectrum falls below the masking thresholds. This scheme, although it ensures transparent watermarks embedding and provide reasonable robustness, faces severe security

Figure 12. Illustration of Savitzky-Golay smoothing filter on one frame, spectrum phase of watermarked audio, smoothed audio and residual audio

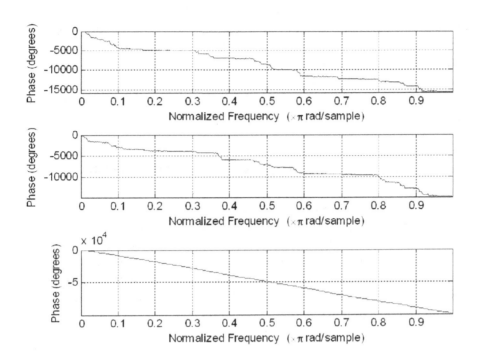

Table 1. New proposed watermarking system robustness tests

Attack\Audio	Country BER (%)	Jazz BER (%)	Pop BER (%)	Rock BER (%)	Classic BER (%)	AVERAGE BER (%)
AWGN SNR=20, 10, 5dB	0	0	0	0	0	0
CNA	0	0	0	0	0	0
LP Filtering	0.08	0.08	0.15	0.79	0.06	0.24
HP Filtering	0.08	0	0.15	0.17	0.12	0.11
BP Filtering	0.55	0.63	1.05	0.34	1.02	0.72
MP3 @ 64 kbps	0	0	0	0.25	0.23	0.10
MP3 @ 32 kbps	0	0	2.40	0.35	0.54	0.66

problems. Any challengers with knowledge of the algorithm can approximate the psychoacoustic model and remove all the components below the masking thresholds, thus eliminating the embedded watermarks and making recovery of the hidden information impossible. The new proposed watermark system, however, improves the system security by embedding watermarks into the entire audio spectrum, whether audible or inaudible. Therefore, it becomes very hard for the opponents to eradicate the watermarks without introducing large amounts of audible distortion to the audio signal, which usually degrades the audio quality so much that makes the audio signal useless.

11.6 MORE WATERMARKING SYSTEMS COMPARISON

In this section, we perform the same comparison as described in previous chapter, i.e. to compare the proposed system to the watermarking system based on the traditional PE based psychoacoustic model. Watermark generation for the PE watermarking system, watermark payload, music materials used for testing and the applied attacks are kept the same as described in previous chapter. The PE watermarking system achieves perfect recovery after it undergoes the more simple attacks that included random cropping, re-sampling, amplitude compression, echo addition and equal-ization. However, errors occurred as a result of noise addition, DA/AD conversion and MPEG compression, and the effects of those attacks were further studied for both system.

We test the same three key parameters in the evaluation of a watermarking scheme: robustness, watermark payload and watermark length.

11.6.1 Watermark Robustness Comparison

In this experiment, we compare the robustness of the proposed system to PE model system.

Both watermarking systems have the same watermark payload of 8.4 bps and the same watermark length of 131072 samples, which spans 2.9722 seconds in the tested music files at 44.1 kHz sampling rate.

The robustness results are listed in Table 2.

Table 2 shows that with the same watermark payload and watermark length the proposed watermarking scheme is more robust and survives better in noise addition, DA/AD conversion and MP3 compression attacks than the PE method.

Table 2. Watermark robustness comparison with PE method

Attack Type	PE Method BER (%)	Proposed Method BER (%)
Noise Addition	3.0	0
DA/AD Conversion	1.5	0
MP3 64 kbps Compression	3.5	0.1

11.6.2 Watermark Payload Comparison

In this experiment, we attempted to insert more useful information in the watermarks in the proposed system while maintaining the same watermark length for both approaches.

The PE model system remains with 8.4 bps watermark payload and 131072 samples long watermark length. On the other hand, the proposed watermarking system employs the same length of watermark, embeds 208 bits information into each audio clip, achieving 10.4 bps watermark payload, which is 24% higher than the PE model system.

The obtained robustness results are depicted in Table 3.

From Table 3, we can clearly see that although the proposed system obtained a much higher watermark payload, it still demonstrates similar robustness compared to the PE model.

11.6.3 Watermark Length Comparison

During this experiment, we try to achieve in the proposed watermarking system the same watermark robustness with the same watermark payload but a shorter length watermark compared to the PE model system.

The PE model system is the same as in Section 9.3.3, which has 8.4 bps watermark payload with 131072 samples long watermark length, the proposed system, on the other hand, realizes 8.4 bps watermark payload with a 65536 samples long

Table 3. Watermark payload comparison with PE method

Attack Type	PE Method BER (%) (8.4 bps)	Proposed Method BER (%) (10.4 bps)
Noise Addition	3.0	0.5
DA/AD Conversion	1.5	0.8
MP3 64 kbps Compression	3.5	2.4

Table 4. Watermark length comparison with PE method

Attack Type	PE Method BER (%) (131072 samples)	Proposed Method BER (%) (65536 samples)
Noise Addition	3.0	1.6
DA/AD Conversion	1.5	0.9
MP3 64 kbps Compression	3.5	2.5

watermark, which is only the half length of the one incorporated in the PE model. The robustness results are shown in Table 4.

From Table 4, we can easily see that the proposed watermark system provides better watermark robustness to the PE model with the same watermark payload, but 50% shorter watermark.

11.7 CONCLUSION

In this chapter, we further enhanced the watermarking system by embedding watermarks to the entire host audio spectrum, whether its power spectrum is below or above the masking thresholds. The watermark strength is carefully tuned to be less than the masking thresholds, which is also referred as just noticeable distortion, thus avoiding introducing audible distortion into the watermarked audio. During the decoding phase, the input audio is segmented into frames and pre-processed by Savitzky-Golay smooth filter to decrease the correlation of the host audio signal. The matched filter is applied on the residual signal to locate the synchronization code and recover the embedded watermarks. The enhanced watermarking scheme performs better than the previously proposed system in terms of system robustness and provides faster decoding process due to the dropping off of psychoacoustic model as well as more security since watermark embedded into the audible audio areas are hard to remove without severely degrading the audio quality. We also compared the enhanced model with the PE model based watermarking system from three perspectives: watermark robustness, watermark payload and watermark length. The experimental results show that the enhanced system beat the PE model based watermarking system in all the perspectives.

REFERENCES

Cvejic, N. (2004). *Algorithms for audio watermarking and steganography* (Unpublished doctoral dissertation). University of Oulu, Oulu, Finland. Retrieved from http://herkules.oulu.fi/ isbn9514273842/ isbn9514273842.pdf

Swanson, M. D., Zhu, B., Tewfik, A. H., & Boney, L. (1998). Robust audio watermarking using perceptual masking. *Elsevier Signal Processing, Special Issue on Copyright Protection and Access Control, 66*(3), 337–355.

William, H. P., Saul, A. T., William, T. V., & Brian, P. F. (1992). *Numerical Recipes in C*. Cambridge, UK: Cambridge University Press.

Chapter 12
A Fast and Precise Synchronization Method for Digital Audio Watermarking

Synchronization is the fundamental problem that most watermarking systems have to deal with. This chapter focuses on research on the synchronization problem. The literature review of traditional synchronization solutions is presented first followed by a proposed fast and precise synchronization method based on distribution of the high energy in the signal.

12.1 INTRODUCTION

The most effective watermarking method is the spread spectrum algorithm, which spreads the pseudo randomly modulated watermarks over the whole spectrum of

DOI: 10.4018/978-1-61520-925-5.ch012

the host signal, making them robust and imperceptible. Linear correlation the watermarked signal with the same PN sequence in the detection process will locate the start of the watermarks in the host signal. Although the payload is usually much lower than other technique, spread spectrum is involved in most of the watermarking systems due to its high robustness (Cox et al., 1997; Cvejic et al., 2001, 2003-b).

In spite of its attractive properties, direct sequence spread spectrum (DSSS), as all other methods, faces the same challenge at the detection side: synchronization. In order to recover the embedded watermark from the stego-signal (watermarked signal), the decoder has to know the beginning location of the embedded watermark first. In another words, the detector has to synchronize with the encoder.

As explained in Section 12.2, current synchronization methods cannot meet the requirements of some applications where a fast, robust and precise synchronization is needed. Therefore, we present in this chapter a synchronization method that is fast, robust, precise and secure, thus meeting the requirements of the watermarking applications that require a real time, computational economy, reliable, accurate and attack-proof synchronization solution.

The rest of the chapter is organized as follows. In Section 12.2, the synchronization problem and classic solutions are illustrated. In the following section, the proposed fast, robust, precise and secure synchronization method is demonstrated in detail. The experiment results are listed in Section 12.4, which support our claims for the novel synchronization method. The conclusion is in Section 12.5.

12.2 THE SYNCHRONIZATION PROBLEM IN WATERMARKING AND TRADITIONAL SOLUTIONS

In this section, the synchronization problem in audio watermarking is illustrated first followed by the traditional solutions.

12.2.1 Synchronization Problem in Audio Watermarking

Due to the similarities between watermarking and communication, the watermarking channel is usually modeled as a conventional communication channel (Cox et al., 2002) as shown in Figure 1.

Suppose the message to be transmitted is m, which is usually modulated to the watermark w and the cover signal is x, then the watermarked signal s is

$$s = x + aw \tag{12.1}$$

Figure 1. Typical watermarking system

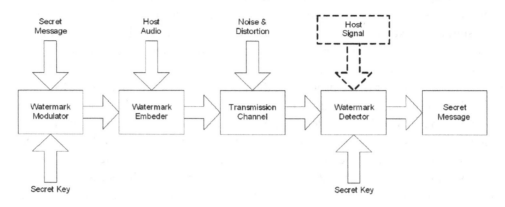

where a is a factor between 0 and 1 controlling watermark strength to prevent introducing perceptible distortion.

There are two types of detectors at the watermark detection side, blind detector where the original host signal is not available for detection, and informed detector, where the host signal is accessible during the detection phase, as indicated by the broken box and arrows in Figure 1. Correlation between received signal and the watermark is performed and a high value of the correlation denotes the existence of watermark. Suppose the length of watermark is N and the channel noise introduced during the transmission is n, then the received signal r is

$$r = s + n = x + aw + n \qquad (12.2)$$

and the correlation between r and w is

$$
\begin{aligned}
c &= \frac{1}{N}\sum_i r_i w_i \\
&= \frac{1}{N}\sum_i x_i w_i + \frac{1}{N}\sum_i a w_i^2 + \frac{1}{N}\sum_i n_i w_i \\
&= d_x + d_w + d_n
\end{aligned}
\qquad (12.3)
$$

Assuming N is sufficiently large, watermark w, host signal x and noise n are independent and Gaussian distributed. Then

$$d_x \approx 0 \; and \; d_n \approx 0 \qquad (12.4)$$

The optimized threshold for watermark detection is chosen as

$$\tau = \frac{1}{2} d_w \qquad (12.5)$$

There are two detection errors that occur, namely false positive error and false negative error. The former denotes the situation when the detector claims the existence of a watermark in an un-watermarked signal section and the latter denotes the opposite. Suppose the probability for false positive and false negative are P_{fp} and P_{fn} respectively and the threshold is chosen as in Equation (12.5), then (Kim, 2003)

$$P_{fp} = P_{fn} = \frac{1}{2} erfc \left(\frac{d_w}{2\sqrt{2}\sigma_r} \right) \qquad (12.6)$$

where σ_r is the standard deviation of the received signal r and erfc() is the complementary error function defined as

$$erfc(x) = \frac{1}{\sqrt{2\pi}} \int_x^\infty e^{\frac{-t^2}{2}} \, dt \qquad (12.7)$$

During the recovery process, the detector needs to know the starting location of the watermark in the received signal. This brings up the synchronization issue. The above Equation (12.3) holds only when the received signal is perfectly aligned with the watermark, in other words, when signal r is synchronized with watermark w, correlation c will reach its maximum. A typical result of c is illustrated in Figure 2. Note in Figure 2, the location of the peak is the beginning of the embedded watermark.

12.2.2 Overview of Traditional Solutions

This section will give a brief overview of the classical solutions developed thus far to solve the synchronization problem.

Figure 2. Typical result of the correlation output

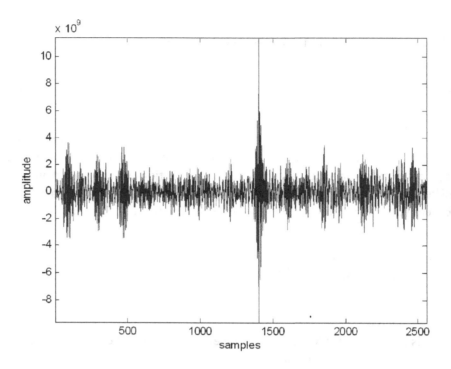

12.2.2.1 Exhaustive Search

An intuitive solution to synchronization is exhaustive search in the received signal, which takes into account all the possible attacks the signal might have undergone during the transmission process, inverses those attack effects followed by the watermark detection. Although this solution works for few applications where the search space is limited, it is not possible for the most real-time needed applications. Moreover, false positive error goes up as the search space increases, which makes it useless for most applications where a low false positive error rate is usually required (Lichtenauer et al., 2003; Licks et al.,2003).

12.2.2.2 Redundant Watermark

If watermarks are repeated N times before embedding in the audio it will have a better chance to achieve synchronization at the detection side. The idea was presented by Kirovski et al. (2001) and it is illustrated as follows:

Figure 3. Example given in Kirovski et al. (2001) to illustrate the redundant chip embedding method

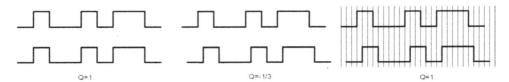

In Figure 3, the leftmost subfigure shows perfect synchronization between the watermark and the received signal during detection where the normalized correlation value is $Q = 1$. The middle subfigure depicts the situation where the watermark is shifted by one sample due to de-synchronization attacks and the normalized correlation is now

$Q = -1/3$, which is a large change from the leftmost subfigure. In rightmost subfigure, the watermark is repeated 3 times before embedding. The normalized correlation is performed only at the center sample of each region and result a high value of $Q = 1$ despite the one chip shift de-synchronization. It is clear that the correlation is correct as long as the linear shift is less than *floor(N/2)* samples. The drawback of the method is that the watermark capacity is reduced by *N* times.

12.2.2.3 Invariant Domain Embedding

Another idea for synchronization is to embed the watermark in a special domain that is invariant to the possible attacks that the signal may encounter.

Such idea was first implemented in image watermarking. In (Ruandaidh et al.,1998) and (Lin et al.,2000), the authors proposed several watermarking systems in the Fourier-Mellin domain and claimed robustness to rotation, scale and translation.

The process of performing Fourier-Mellin transform includes three steps (Licks et al., 2005). First the Discrete Fourier transform (DFT) is performed on the signal. Then the DFT magnitude spectrum is transformed into a log-polar mapping followed by a second DFT transform.

One of the earliest attempts of introducing Fourier-Mellin transform into audio watermarking / fingerprinting happened in (Seo et al., 2002) for a proposed linear speed-change resilient audio fingerprinting based on the Fourier-Mellin transform. They claimed their scale invariance audio fingerprinting algorithm to be robust against the speed change up to ±10%.

12.2.2.4 Using Synchronization Marks

Synchronization marks are codes with special features known both to the encoder and decoder. They usually don't carry any watermark information and are used only for synchronization purposes. The detector can use the known feature of those marks to perform an exhaustive search to achieve synchronization and keep the false positive error rate low. A pseudo random (PN) sequence is widely used for the synchronization marks for its well know good autocorrelation property. (Cox et al., 2002; Bender et al., 1996; Cox et al., 1997).

Several authors (Garcia, 1999; Jung et al., 2003) have used PN sequence as synchronization marks for audio watermarking and achieved some robustness against the de-synchronization attack. Synchronization marks, however, have their own limitations. They compromise the watermark capacity since they do not carry any watermark information. They also bring up the watermark security problem since the opponents can guess the PN sequence and perform template estimation attacks. (Gomes, 2001)

12.2.2.5 Using Self-Synchronized Watermarks

In order to solve the problems brought by synchronization marks, self-synchronized watermarks are used for watermarking. Those watermarks are specially designed so that the autocorrelation of the watermarks have one or several peaks, thus achieving synchronization (Licks et al., 2005).

Although people have reported successful synchronization using self-synchronized watermarks (Kutter, 1998; Delannay, et al., 2000), this method is also susceptible to estimation attacks. The opponent, once the watermark is known, can perform an autocorrelation between the watermarked signal and the watermark, remove all the periodic peaks and make the detection of the watermark fail.

12.2.2.6 Feature Points or Content Synchronization

Feature points synchronization, which also referred to as salient points or content based synchronization, is regarded as the second generation synchronization method (Bas et al., 2002). Feature points are the stable sections of the host signal that are invariant or nearly invariant against the common signal processing or attacks. The feature points are extracted both at the encoder and decoder side to achieve synchronization (Bas et al., 2002).

Wu et al. (1999 and 2000) presented a robust audio watermarking using audio content analysis. The feature points in their methods are defined as the fast energy climbing area, which are perceptually important, thus stable during the normal signal processing. Those feature points can survive many malicious attacks as long as signal perceptually transparency is kept.

Kirovski et al. (2002) proposed a robust audio watermarking system robust to de-synchronization via beat detection. The feature points used in this method are the beats, which are the most robust events in music signals. The mean beat period of the music is estimated during the embedding process and watermarks are inserted at onset of the beat. The detector first extracts the mean beat period and locates the onset of the beat, thus synchronizes with the watermark.

In (Li et al., 2003), the signal is first decomposed by discrete wavelet transform (DWT) and the statistical features in the wavelet domain are employed as the feature points. The mean of the wavelet coefficient values at the coarsest approximation sub band provides information about the low frequency distribution of the audio signal (Tzanetakis et al., 2001), which represents the mostly perceptual components of the signal and is relatively stable after common signal processing (Li et al.,2003). This mean is adopted as the feature points for synchronization purpose in their system.

A feature points based synchronization method does not need to embed extra marks for synchronization, which saves the watermark capacity and introduces less distortion to the host signal. However, it is very hard for this method to achieve accurate sample-to-sample synchronization.

12.3 A FAST AND EFFICIENT SYNCHRONIZATION METHOD

Although many synchronization methods have been proposed in the literature as mentioned in the previous section, they are either complicated (Ruandaidh et al.,1998; Lin et al.,2000; Seo et al.,2002)(exhaustive search, invariant domain embedding), not secure (Garcia, 1999; Jung et al.,2003; Gomes, 2001; Kutter, 1998; Delannay, et al., 2000) (synchronization marks or self synchronized watermark), or not precise (Wu et al., 1999; Wu et al.,2000 ; Kirovski, et al.,2003; Li et al.,2003; Tzanetakis et al.,2001) (feature points synchronization). When facing applications which require a fast, robust and precise synchronization, a better than classical synchronization method is needed.

In this section, we propose a novel synchronization algorithm that meets the following goals:

a. *Fast*, which makes the real-time synchronization possible.
b. *Robust*, which makes the synchronization reliable under common signal processing or even attacks.
c. *Precise*, which enables sample-to-sample synchronization possible.

d.   *Secure*, which deters the common estimation attack against guessing the location of the PN sequence.

This novel synchronization algorithm is composed of three major parts: feature points extraction, PN sequence scrambling and matched filter detection.

12.3.1 Feature Points Extraction

Similar to the idea presented in Section 12.2.2.6, we also employed feature points as our synchronization method.

In order to achieve fast synchronization to meet real-time requirement, the feature points should be chosen in the way that they can be extracted easily with cheap computational cost. In our method, we use the distribution of high energy areas as our feature points.

The high energy areas are the perceptual important components of the audio and they are very stable after common signal processing, including mp3 compression. If those areas have been changed too much, obvious audible distortion will be introduced the audio and makes it sound annoying.

Consider the audio signal x(n) of N samples, the procedure of high energy area extraction goes as follows (He et al., 2008-a).

The average signal energy is calculated using the following equation

$$x_{avg} = \frac{\sum_{i=1}^{N} x^2(i)}{N} \tag{12.8}$$

The signal is segmented into non-overlapping blocks each contains L samples. Let $M = floor(\frac{N}{L})$, where *floor(x)* is the function rounds x towards minus infinity, then M is the number of blocks in audio signal *x(n)*.

The average signal energy of each block is calculated. Let *x(i,j)* denotes the *jth* sample in the *ith* block, then the average signal energy of *ith* block is calculated as

$$avg_i = \frac{\sum_{j=1}^{L} x^2(i,j)}{L} \tag{12.9}$$

Energy threshold is got by multiply the average signal energy with a secrete factor α, which is known both to encoder and decoder. Let T denotes the energy threshold, then

$$T = \alpha x_{avg} \qquad\qquad (12.10)$$

Record the location and length of each high energy section by the following pseudo code:

```
HEngLoc = zeros(1,M)
LenHEngLoc = zeros(1,M)
index = 1;
Eng_Ch_Inx = 1;
for i = 1 to M
        if avg_i >= T
                if Eng_Ch_Inx = 1
                        HEngLoc(index) = i;
                        Eng_Ch_Inx = 0;
                            end
                LenHEngLoc(index)++;
        end
        else
                index++;
                Eng_Ch_Inx = 1;
        end
end
```

In the above code, HEngLoc records the start location of each high energy areas and LengHEngLoc records the length of each high energy area. Index denotes the number of high energy areas and the Eng_Ch_Inx denotes the change between high and low energy areas. The longest K high energy areas are chosen as the features points for synchronization. The factor K is defined according to the watermarking application requirements.

In the decoder side, the same procedure is performed to locate all the high energy areas (as well as their neighbor blocks) which are later correlated with the PN sequence to achieve synchronization purpose. As we can see later from the experimental results, the locations of high energy areas are very stable under the normal signal processing as well as malicious attacks.

The secrete factor α in Equation (12.10) controls the high energy blocks distribution. Different α results different high energy blocks distribution. A lower α decreases the thresholds for high energy areas, thus more areas are treated as high energy area. Although this provides more room to embed the watermarks, it reduces the system robustness since some high energy areas may become unstable after common signal processing or attacks. A higher α, on the other hand, increases such threshold, thus decreasing the number of high energy areas. Better robustness is achieved at the cost of less capacity for watermark embedding. By keeping this factor secret, the system deters the attackers from guessing the locations of high energy distribution used between encoder and decoder, thus making the synchronization method more secure.

12.3.2 PN Sequence Scrambling and Multiple PN Sequences Embedding

A PN sequence is used to implement the synchronization in our method. However, the PN sequence employed is carefully designed to meet the following goals:

- The length of the PN sequence should be as short as possible to avoid introducing audible noise but long enough to achieve robust correlation (Gomes, 2001).
- The strength of the PN sequence should be adaptive to the host signal energy so a stronger PN sequence could be used to achieve better robustness while keeping the introduced distortion under the perceptible level (Cox et al., 2002).
- The PN sequence should be hard to guess to mitigate the estimation attacks.

In order to meet the above goals, the PN sequence employed in our system has the some special features.

The PN sequence is 2560 samples long, or about 58ms for 44.1 kHz sampling rate audio.

This length is long enough to achieve robust synchronization and short enough to avoid introducing audible noise as well as hard to estimate for attackers.

To further improve the security of the PN sequence and mitigate the estimation attacks, the PN sequence is scrambled before adding to the host signal. The purpose of scrambling is to make guessing the PN sequence very difficult while scrambled marks still keeping the good autocorrelation property of the PN sequence.

In order to take the advantage of temporal masking phenomena in psychoacoustic model, the PN sequence is embedded in the high energy area, start from the beginning of the high energy blocks with some fixed offset. Let *pn* be the PN sequence,

Figure 4. Synchronization system illustration

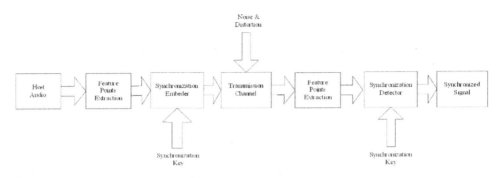

x(n) be the host signal and *S(n)* be the host signal with embedded PN sequence, then (Kim, 2003)

$$S(i) = x(i) + cpn(i) \tag{12.11}$$

where *c* is a factor adaptively controls the strength of PN sequence to meet both the robustness and inaudibility requirements.

For some watermarking applications, multiple watermarks are embedded in the host signal to protect different information. For instance, the system may embed one watermark representing the author's name and use another watermark to embed the author's signature which may be a small graph (Cox et al., 2002). This brings up the problem of multiple watermarking synchronization. Fortunately, due to the orthogonality of the PN sequence (Cox et al., 1997), multiple different PN sequences can be embedded using the proposed method to solve this problem. We will show how to do this in the experimental results section.

12.3.3 Matched Filter Detection

Matched filter is used in our method to detect the existence of the PN sequence and precisely locate the starting sample of the PN sequence.

The detailed information about matched filter has been explained in Chapter 10. The whole synchronization system is illustrated in Figure 4.

12.4 EXPERIMENTAL RESULTS

A set of five audio files was used to evaluate the novel synchronization method. They contained varying musical pieces of CD-quality that included jazz, classical, pop, country and rock music, each about 20 seconds long.

Several attacks are applied on the proposed synchronization system to test the robustness and they include:

a. *Random cropping:* Samples are randomly deleted or added to the watermarked audio.
b. *White noise addition:* White Gaussian noise was added to the watermarked audio for an average SNR of 20 dB.
c. *Re-sampling:* The watermarked audio is down sampled to 22.05 kHz and then up sampled to 44.1 kHz.
d. *DA / AD conversion:* The watermarked audio is played on the computer and the output is recorded through the line-in jack on the sound card of the same computer.
e. *MPEG compression:* The watermarked audio is compressed into mp3 format at various bit rates and then decompressed back into wave file.

Three experiments were made to test our ideas in the synchronization method, which include robustness of high energy distribution, single PN sequence embedding for synchronization and multiple PN sequence embedding for synchronization.

12.4.1 Robustness of High Energy Distribution

As we stated in section 12.3, the high energy distribution is stable and robust against normal signal processing and attacks. This experiment validates our claim.

As for the above mentioned attacks, MPEG compression is the most widely used attack to scramble the synchronization and can cause the worst result among the above attacks.

We choose the country music as an example to show that the high energy distribution is robust against MPEG compression. Using other audio files will give similar results. The high energy distribution of the country music before and after 64 kbps MPEG compression are listed in Table 1 and shown in Figure 5 and Figure 6 respectively.

As we can see from the Table 1 and Figure 5 and Figure 6, high energy block locations are very stable and changes very little after mp3 compression. Longer high energy blocks are much robust than shorter ones. Some very short high energy blocks even becomes missing after mp3 compression (denoted as "None" in

Table 1. Robustness test for high energy blocks distribution

Before MP3 Compression		After MP3 compression		Location Offset
Block Location	**Block Length**	**Block Location**	**Block Length**	
10	5	10	6	0
25	8	26	7	1
46	2	46	2	0
51	1	None	None	/
57	3	58	3	1
82	3	82	4	0
90	7	90	7	0
109	3	110	2	1
121	1	122	1	0
137	3	138	5	1
141	2	None	None	/
145	2	145	2	0
153	10	154	9	1
173	7	173	7	0
205	4	205	5	0
217	13	217	13	0
266	26	266	27	0
296	22	296	23	0
329	7	329	8	0
337	2	338	1	1

the table). Therefore, the PN sequence is only embedded in high energy blocks with length higher than 5 blocks. During the detection, the system searches around the high energy locations within ±5 blocks range and achieves the precise sample-to-sample synchronization.

12.4.2 Single Watermarking Synchronization

To test the robustness of the synchronization method against above attacks, one PN sequence of 2560 samples is adaptively embedded into each of the audio signal. Under some attacks (DA / AD conversion, MPEG compression) where an unknown delay is usually introduced into the audio signal, a all '1' mark sequence with high energy (to ensure the detection) is embedded into the audio signal with a fixed off-set (20000 samples in the experiments) from the PN sequence. If after detection,

Figure 5. Original high energy block distribution

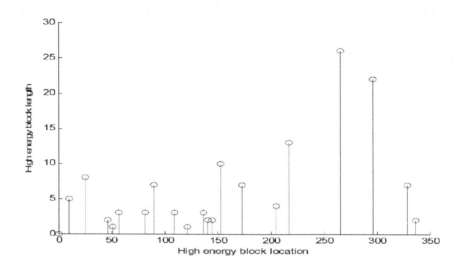

Figure 6. High energy block distribution after mp3 compression

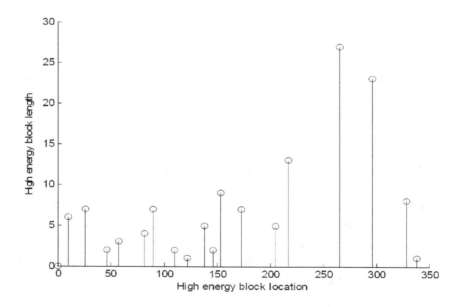

Table 2. Synchronization robustness test for single watermarking system

Audio	Location	RC	NA	RS	DA/AD	MC
Country	Before	682240	682240	682240	20000	20000
	After	692240	682240	682240	20000	20000
	Offset	10000	0	0	0	0
Jazz	Before	454400	454400	454400	20000	20000
	After	464400	454400	454400	20000	20000
	Offset	10000	0	0	0	0
Pop	Before	96000	96000	96000	20000	20000
	After	106000	96000	96000	20000	20000
	Offset	10000	0	0	0	0
Rock	Before	480000	480000	480000	20000	20000
	After	490000	480000	480000	20000	20000
	Offset	10000	0	0	0	0
Classic	Before	216320	216320	216320	20000	20000
	After	226320	216320	216320	20000	20000
	Offset	10000	0	0	0	0

Note for Table 2:

RC: Random cropping

NA: Noise addition

RS: Re-sampling

DA/AD: DA / AD conversion

MC: MPEG compression

Before: Original PN sequence location. For RC, NA and RS, the PN sequence location before attacks. For DA/AD and MC, the distance between PN sequence and mark sequence before attacks.

After: For RC, NA and RS, the PN sequence location after attacks. For DA/AD and MC, the distance between PN sequence and mark sequence after attacks.

Offset: The difference between "before" and "after" locations.

the offset between those two sequences remains the same as in the encoder side, a sample-to-sample synchronization is considered successfully accomplished.

Table 2 contains the results for the synchronization robustness test under those attacks.

In the random cropping test, 10000 samples are randomly added into the host signal before the embedded PN sequence. Other cropping attacks, including deleting samples before the embedded PN sequence, adding or deleting samples after the embedded PN sequence, show similar results. The offset of 10000 samples after attack demonstrates a successful sample-to-sample synchronization.

For DA / AD conversion and MPEG compression, as we can see from Table 2, the fixed offset of 20000 samples between PN sequence and the mark sequence proves the robustness against those attacks.

12.4.3 Multiple Watermarking Synchronization

In some applications, multiple watermarks are required to protect different information (author's name, signature, etc.). This brings up the issue of multiple watermarking synchronization. The proposed method solved this issue using the orthogonality of PN sequences.

Two different PN sequences are embedded in each of the audio files and undergo above attacks. The results are shown in Table 3

From Table 3 we can see

For RC, NA and RS test, both PN sequences have achieved perfect synchronization.

For DA / AD and MPEG compression, different offsets do show in the results. However, all the offsets for PN1 and PN2 remains the same, which mean those off-sets are the delay introduced by the attacks and the system still demonstrate perfect sample-to-sample synchronization. We can also see that the MPEG compression introduced a fixed 1201 samples delay to all the audio signals.

During further experiments, more PN sequences (three and above) are embedded in those audio files with the proposed method. Similar results show the perfect sample-to-sample synchronization has been attained.

Informal listening test shows that no perceptual distortion can be heard after embedding the synchronization marks into the host audio, which means the synchronization method is transparent.

We also tested this synchronization method on speech signals with sapling rate down to 8 kHz and got similar promising results, which makes this method appropriate for speech watermarking.

12.4.4 Multiple Watermarking Synchronization Under Time Scaling Attack

For more severe attacks such as time scaling attack, the length of the audio could change a lot, which causes the above synchronization method fail to locate the embedded PN sequence.

In the time scaling scenario, the exact stamped sample may be removed which makes locating such sample impossible. The goal for synchronization here is to find a position that is close to the assuming location.

Table 3. Synchronization robustness test for multiple watermarking system

Audio	PN	Location	RC	NA	RS	DA/AD	MC
Country	PN1	Before	682240	682240	682240	682240	682240
		After	692240	682240	682240	683250	683441
		Offset	10000	0	0	1010	1201
	PN2	Before	759040	759040	759040	759040	759040
		After	769040	759040	759040	760050	760241
		Offset	10000	0	0	1010	1201
Jazz	PN1	Before	454400	454400	454400	454400	454400
		After	464400	454400	454400	455515	455601
		Offset	10000	0	0	1115	1201
	PN2	Before	559360	559360	559360	559360	559360
		After	569360	559360	559360	560475	560561
		Offset	10000	0	0	1115	1201
Pop	PN1	Before	96000	96000	96000	96000	96000
		After	106000	96000	96000	97303	97201
		Offset	10000	0	0	1303	1201
	PN2	Before	116480	116480	116480	116480	116480
		After	126480	116480	116480	117783	117681
		Offset	10000	0	0	1303	1201
Rock	PN1	Before	480000	480000	480000	480000	480000
		After	490000	480000	480000	481453	481201
		Offset	10000	0	0	1453	1201
	PN2	Before	702720	702720	702720	702720	702720
		After	712720	702720	702720	704173	703921
		Offset	10000	0	0	1453	1201
Classic	PN1	Before	216320	216320	216320	216320	216320
		After	226320	216320	216320	217402	217521
		Offset	10000	0	0	1082	1201
	PN2	Before	259840	259840	259840	259840	259840
		After	269840	259840	259840	260922	261041
		Offset	10000	0	0	1082	1201

Figure 7. Typical set of received signal, approximated signal and residual signal

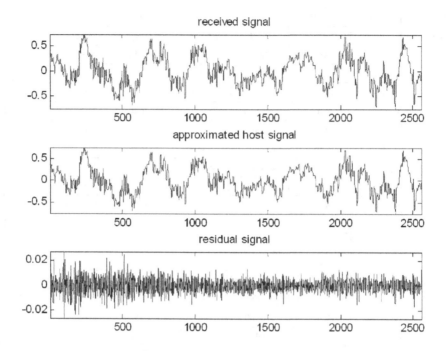

In order to minimize the interference of the host audio and improve detection precision, we first try to remove the host signal from the received signal and apply the matched filter to the residual signal. The process goes as follows:

Suppose the received signal is

$$y = x + w + n \tag{12.17}$$

Where x is the host audio, w is the PN sequence and n is possible noise, the residual signal is calculated as:

$$r = y - f(y) \tag{12.18}$$

Where $f(y)$ is the approximated host signal obtained by applying Savitzky-Golay smoothing filters on the received signal.

Table 4. Time scaling (95% to 99%) test for multiple watermarking system

Audio	PN	Location	TS 95%	TS 96%	TS 97%	TS 98%	TS 99%
Country	PN1	Before	682240	682240	682240	682240	682240
		After	650312	656275	662918	669359	675543
		Error Rate (%)	0.32	0.19	0.17	0.11	0
	PN2	Before	695040	695040	695040	695040	695040
		After	661516	667825	674653	681087	688343
		Error Rate (%)	0.18	0.08	0.07	0.01	0.04
Jazz	PN1	Before	454400	454400	454400	454400	454400
		After	432158	439498	441307	448384	452757
		Error Rate (%)	0.11	0.72	0.12	0.68	0.64
	PN2	Before	467200	467200	467200	467200	467200
		After	445324	449022	453394	460102	462994
		Error Rate (%)	0.32	0.11	0.04	0.48	0.10
Pop	PN1	Before	65280	65280	65280	65280	65280
		After	61909	62734	63414	63202	64189
		Error Rate (%)	0.16	0.10	0.14	1.18	0.67
	PN2	Before	78080	78080	78080	78080	78080
		After	73813	74974	75317	76002	76989
		Error Rate (%)	0.46	0.02	0.54	0.66	0.40
Rock	PN1	Before	480000	480000	480000	480000	480000
		After	457357	461869	468966	470922	475180
		Error Rate (%)	0.28	0.22	0.70	0.11	0
	PN2	Before	492800	492800	492800	492800	492800
		After	469365	476037	478005	482929	487980
		Error Rate (%)	0.24	0.60	0	0	0.02
Classic	PN1	Before	216320	216320	216320	216320	216320
		After	207950	210007	212386	213989	216575
		Error Rate (%)	1.13	1.08	1.18	0.92	1.12
	PN2	Before	229120	229120	229120	229120	229120
		After	217742	219797	221727	224229	226366
		Error Rate (%)	0.03	0.07	0.23	0.13	0.20

Table 5. Time scaling (101% to 105%) test for multiple watermarking system

Audio	PN	Location	TS 101%	TS 102%	TS 103%	TS 104%	TS 105%
Country	PN1	Before	682240	682240	682240	682240	682240
		After	688665	696579	703528	712808	718472
		Error Rate (%)	0.05	0.10	0.12	0.48	0.31
	PN2	Before	695040	695040	695040	695040	695040
		After	702341	709379	716328	723762	731272
		Error Rate (%)	0.05	0.06	0.06	0.13	0.21
Jazz	PN1	Before	454400	454400	454400	454400	454400
		After	458611	463687	468258	472869	480357
		Error Rate (%)	0.07	0.04	0.05	0.06	0.71
	PN2	Before	467200	467200	467200	467200	467200
		After	472128	476124	481063	486402	491668
		Error Rate (%)	0.05	0.09	0.03	0.11	0.24
Pop	PN1	Before	65280	65280	65280	65280	65280
		After	65249	66236	67056	67332	68330
		Error Rate (%)	1.00	0.54	0.28	0.86	0.33
	PN2	Before	78080	78080	78080	78080	78080
		After	78049	79036	79856	81033	81130
		Error Rate (%)	1.04	0.78	0.73	0.22	1.09
Rock	PN1	Before	480000	480000	480000	480000	480000
		After	484643	489821	494215	502546	507518
		Error Rate (%)	0.03	0.05	0.04	0.70	0.73
	PN2	Before	492800	492800	492800	492800	492800
		After	497443	502621	507410	512786	518556
		Error Rate (%)	0.06	0.01	0.04	0.06	0.23
Classic	PN1	Before	216320	216320	216320	216320	216320
		After	220807	222979	224778	227857	229948
		Error Rate (%)	1.02	1.08	0.91	1.33	1.30
	PN2	Before	229120	229120	229120	229120	229120
		After	231495	233220	235914	238545	241091
		Error Rate (%)	0.04	0.21	0.03	0.11	0.22

Table 6. Average error rate due to time scaling attack

Attack	Average Error Rate (%)
TS 95%	0.323
TS 96%	0.319
TS 97%	0.319
TS 98%	0.427
TS 99%	0.315
TS 101%	0.341
TS 102%	0.296
TS 103%	0.229
TS 104%	0.406
TS 105%	0.537

A typical set of the received signal, approximated host signal and residual signal are illustrated in Figure 7. We can see from Figure 7, the residual signal is more noise like and the experimental results show that a better detection performance is achieved by the above process.

The same five audio files are used for time scaling evaluation. Two watermarks are randomly embedded into each file which then undergoes time scaling attack with scaling factor from 0.99 to 1.05. The decoder then tries to locate the watermarks from the distorted signal and the results are shown in Table 4, 5 and 6.

The error rate is calculated as follows

If the original location of the stamped sample is N, the time scaling factor is a, then the correct location after scaling is N*a, the detected location is M, then:

$$err = abs(\frac{M}{N} - a) \qquad (12.19)$$

As we can see from above tables, the detection error rate is between 0.02% and 0.06%, which is extremely small.

12.5 CONCLUSION

In this chapter, we proposed a fast and precise sample-to-sample synchronization method for audio watermarking. High energy blocks distribution of the host audio is used as the feature points for the synchronization purpose due to its stable property under the common signal processing and attacks. Those feature points are first extracted in the encoder side as the reference to embed the synchronization marks (PN sequence). The synchronization marks are carefully tuned according to the energy of the host signal as well as using the temporal masking phenomena of psychoacoustic model to avoid introducing audible noise. At the decoder side, energy analysis is performed first to locate the high energy blocks. A matched filter is applied around those locations to further trace the location of the synchronization marks, thus achieving a high precise sample-to-sample synchronization.

In order to accommodate the synchronization need for multiple watermarking system, more than one synchronization marks could be embedded into the host audio with the proposed method to accomplish the multiple watermarking synchronization task.

The experimental results show that the proposed synchronization method is fast, robust, precise and secure, which is perfect for the watermarking applications that require a real time, computationally economy, reliable, accurate and attack-proof synchronization solution.

When the watermarked signal undergoes a time scaling attack, the stamped sample may be removed which makes the exact detection very hard and sometimes impossible. However, our system still can find the position that is very close to the original locations with error rate less than 0.6%.

REFERENCES

Bas, P., Chassery, J.-M., & Macq, B. (2002). Geometrically invariant watermarking using feature points. *IEEE Transactions on Image Processing, 11*(9), 1014–1028. doi:10.1109/TIP.2002.801587

Bender, W., Gruhl, D., Morimoto, N., & Lu, A. (1996). Techniques for data hiding. *IBM Systems Journal, 35*(3/4), 313–336. doi:10.1147/sj.353.0313

Cox, I. J., Kilian, J., Leighton, T., & Shamoon, T. (1997). Secure spread spectrum watermarking for multimedia. *IEEE Transactions on Image Processing, 6*(12), 1673–1687. doi:10.1109/83.650120

Cox, I. J., Miller, M. L., & Bloom, J. A. (2002). *Digital watermarking*. San Francisco, CA: Academic Press.

Cvejic, N., Keskinarkaus, A., & Seppänen, T. (2001). Audio watermarking using m-sequences and temporal masking. In *Proceedings of the IEEE ASSP Workshop on Applications of Signal Processing to Audio and Acoustics* (pp. 227-230).

Cvejic, N., & Seppänen, T. (2003b). Fusing digital audio watermarking and authentication in diverse signal domains. In *Proceedings of the European Signal Processing Conference* (pp. 84-87). Antalya, Turkey.

Delannay, D., & Macq, B. (2000). Generalized 2D cyclic patterns for secret watermark generation. In []. Vancouver, BC, Canada.]. *Proceedings of the IEEE International Conference of Image Processing, 2*, 72–79.

Garcia, R. A. (1999). Digital watermarking of audio signals using a psychoacoustic model and spread spectrum theory. In *Proceedings of the 107ᵗʰ Convention of Audio Engineering Society (AES)* (Preprint 5073). New York, NY.

Gomes, L. de C. T. (2001). Resynchronization methods for audio watermarking. *Proceedings of the 111ᵗʰ Convention of Audio Engineering Society (AES)* (Preprint 5441). New York, NY.

He, X., & Scordilis, M. M. (2008a). Efficiently synchronized spread spectrum audio watermarking. *Research Letters in Signal Processing*. doi:10.1155/2008/251868

Jung, S., Seok, J., & Hong, J. (2003). An improved detection technique for spread spectrum audio watermarking with a spectral envelope filter. *ETRI, 25*(1), 52–54. doi:10.4218/etrij.03.0203.0103

Kim, H. J. (2003). Audio watermarking techniques. In *Proceedings of the Pacific Rim Workshop on Digital Steganography*. Kitakyushu, Japan.

Kirovski, D., & Attias, H. (2002). Audio watermark robustness to de-synchronization via beat detection. In *Proceedings of the 5ᵗʰ International Workshop on Information Hiding*. Noordwijkerhout, Netherlands (pp. 160-176).

Kirovski, D., & Malvar, H. S. (2001). Robust spread-spectrum audio watermarking. In *Proceedings of the IEEE International Conference on Acoustics, Speech and Signal Processing (ICASSP)* (3, pp. 1345-1348). Salt Lake City, UT.

Kirovski, D., & Malvar, H. S. (2003). Spread-spectrum watermarking of audio signals. *IEEE Transactions on Signal Processing, 51*(4), 1020–1033. doi:10.1109/TSP.2003.809384

Kutter, M. (1998). Watermarking resisting to translation, rotation, and scaling. In []. Boston, MA.]. *Proceedings of the SPIE Multimedia Systems and Applications, 3528*, 423–431.

Li, W., & Xue, X. (2003). An audio watermarking technique that is robust against random cropping. *Computer Music Journal, 27*(4), 58–68. doi:10.1162/014892603322730505

Lichtenauer, J., Setyawan, I., Kalker, T., & Lagendijk, R. (2003). Exhaustive geometrical search and false positive watermark detection probability. In *Proceedings of the SPIE Electronic Imaging, Security and Watermarking of Multimedia Contents* (4, pp. 203-214). Santa Clara, CA.

Licks, V., & Jordan, R. (2005). Geometric attacks on image watermarking systems. *IEEE MultiMedia, 12*(3), 68–78. doi:10.1109/MMUL.2005.46

Lin, C.-Y., Bloom, J. A., Cox, I. J., Miller, M. L., & Liu, Y. M. (2000). Rotation, scale and translation-resilient public watermarking for images. In *Proceedings of the SPIE Security Watermarking Multimedia Contents II, 3971*, 90–98.

Ruandaidh, J. J. K. O., & Pun, T. (1998). Rotation, scale and translation invariant spread spectrum digital image watermarking. *Signal Processing, 66*, 303–317. doi:10.1016/S0165-1684(98)00012-7

Tzanetakis, G., Essl, G., & Cook, P. (2001). Audio analysis using the discrete wavelet transforms. In *Proceedings of the International Conference of Acoustics and Music: Theory and Applications*. Skiathos, Greece. Retrieved from http://www.cs.princeton. edu/ ~gessl/papers/amta2001.pdf.

Wu, C.-P., Su, P.-C., & Kuo, C.-C. J. (1999). Robust audio watermarking for copyright protection. *Proceedings of the Society for Photo-Instrumentation Engineers, 3807*, 387–397.

Wu, C.-P., Su, P.-C., & Kuo, C.-C. J. (2000). Robust and efficient digital audio watermarking using audio content analysis. *Proceedings of the Society for Photo-Instrumentation Engineers, 3971*, 382–392.

Chapter 13
Conclusion and Future Trends

13.1 CONCLUSION OF THE BOOK

In this book, we introduced the advanced techniques and models for signal processing, perceptual coding and watermarking of digital, however with more emphasis
on watermarking technologies. The beginning chapter briefly explains the human
auditory system (HAS) and psychoacoustics followed by the introduction of digital
watermarking in Chapter 2. New applications of digital watermarking are presented
in Chapter 3 and background and literature review of selected watermarking techniques are presented in Chapter 4. Because of the dominant popularity of spread
spectrum used in digital watermarking, Chapter 5 through Chapter 7 demonstrated
this technology in great detail including the principles of spread spectrum, the survey of current audio watermarking schemes based on spread spectrum and several
techniques to improve traditional spread spectrum detection.

Starting from Chapter 8 to the end of the book, we explain in great detail our
major contributions to a better digital audio watermarking solution, including a
novel discrete wavelet packet transform (DWPT) based psychoacoustic model and

DOI: 10.4018/978-1-61520-925-5.ch013

a synchronization method, which are the most fundamental and important keys for a successful digital audio watermarking system.

Due to the great sensitive property of the human auditory system (HAS) compared to the human visual system (HVS), embedding watermarks into audio signal is much more challenging than inserting watermarks into image or video signals. To make the embedding process transparent and provide enjoyable high quality watermarked audio to the listeners, a psychoacoustic model is indispensable to most of the digital audio watermarking systems.

The psychoacoustic model is a stereotype used to exploit the properties of HAS discovered from state-of-the-art results in psychoacoustics research. Such model takes advantage of the so called masking phenomena, which include frequency and temporal masking, to find out the spaces in the audio signal spectrum that fall below the masking thresholds and can be removed without introducing perceptible distortion. Those spaces can be used to embed watermarks for audio watermarking applications or to tolerate increased quantization noise in perceptual audio coding.

Unlike Fourier transform-based psychoacoustic models, which linearly divide the audio spectrum into different frequency sub bands, our proposed psychoacoustic model takes the advantage of the flexibility of the DWPT and decomposes the audio spectrum in the way that the sub bands distribution closely mimics the critical bands. This psychoacoustic model finds more spaces under the masking thresholds compared to the Fourier transform based psychoacoustic model, thus providing possible better robustness for watermarking applications by tolerating higher energy watermarks embedded imperceptibly. Meanwhile, the proposed psychoacoustic model is also attractive for perceptual audio coding by allowing more quantization noise introduced into the audio coding process, thus achieving a lower coding rate, resulting a smaller coded audio file.

Based on the new psychoacoustic model, we propose a high perceptual quality audio coder which proves performs better than MP3 audio codec.

We also incorporate the new proposed psychoacoustic model into a spread spectrum based audio watermarking system, which enables transparent watermarking embedding and provides reasonable robustness against normal signal processing and attacks. Later in Chapter 11, a more advanced watermarking system was further developed by embedding watermarks into the entire audio spectrum, whether audible or inaudible. This novel system carefully tunes the watermark strength according to the masking thresholds derived from the proposed psychoacoustic model, thus avoiding introducing annoying audible distortion into the watermarked audio. Since the watermarks are spread into the whole audio spectrum, it is very hard if not impossible for the opponents to remove the watermarks without severely degrading the audio quality. The enhanced system shows better robustness, offering faster decoding

Another contribution of the book is a new synchronization method presented in Chapter 12. Synchronization is necessary for audio watermarking detector to find out the starting location of the embedded watermarks before it can recover those watermarks. Synchronization is so far one of the weakest link of watermarking techniques. In scrambling attacks, for example, the synchronization, the opponent can easily defeat the watermarking system, making the detection and recovery of the embedded watermarks impossible. By utilizing the stability of high-energy components distribution in the audio signal, we accomplished a fast and efficient synchronization method for watermarking systems. The fast, robust, secure and precise synchronization algorithm is made possible by the combination of the feature points extraction, PN sequence scrambling and matched filter detection. The stability of the high-energy distribution makes the synchronization fast and robust, even after the signal undergoes common signal processing like AD/DA conversion, MP3 audio compression, noise addition, etc. PN sequence scrambling makes the opponents hard to guess the PN sequence used for synchronization, thus providing the security. Matched filter detection in a limited space makes the synchronization precise.

13.2 FUTURE TRENDS

Psychoacoustic Modeling

Current psychoacoustic modeling are based on the approximation of the not fully understood human auditory system, especially the way cochlea works. Perfect psychoacoustic modeling will not become available unless people can find out how exactly the HAS functions. Question such as the masking threshold produced by combining simple maskers (sinusoids or band-limited noise) be predicted from their individual masking thresholds is not so far been answered clearly in published literature. As a simple example of implementation, MPEG standards take the simple sum of the individual masking thresholds.

However, several studies (Green et al., 1967; Lutfi et al., 1983; Humes et al., 1989) have shown that the combined masking effect of two equally effective simultaneous maskers is 3 to 15 dB greater than the masking predicted by the linear addition of masker energies, which is defined as excess masking. How to derive a model for the excess masking, which exists in both frequency and time domain, could be an interesting problem for further investigation.

Another difficulty for current psychoacoustic models is to deal with multi-channel (5.1 or 7.1) audio signals. How precisely the maskers in one channel can produce and affect the masking thresholds in other channels is still a myth to all the current psychoacoustic modeling methods.

Watermark Payload for Spread Spectrum Technology

Compared to some other watermarking schemes such as phase coding, in spread spectrum-based techniques audio watermarking provides for relatively small watermark payload, which means that for the same length of audio, the latter system can only accommodate much a shorter secret message. This limitation makes spread spectrum unsuitable for some applications where large amounts of data hiding is desired (e.g., audio enhancing metadata information.) Due to the nature of spread spectrum technology, where the hidden data is spread over a much large bandwidth spectrum, high capacity watermark payload remains a challenge to be overcome in future research efforts.

Improved Synchronization

Although the proposed synchronization method is robust to lots of common signal processing and malicious attacks, it is not robust to some sophistic malicious attacks like time or frequency scaling to 10%. This is due to the relatively changed sample values and locations after those attacks. The improved method can achieve an extremely low error rate, it is still not error free. Embedding those synchronization PN sequence in the domain that is invariant to those attacks is the further work for synchronization research.

Other Attacks and Signal Transformations

Besides de-synchronization attacks, other attacks could cause trouble for digital audio watermarking system. Those attacks include, but are not limited to, MP3 compression, digital to analog (D/A) and analog to digital (A/D) conversion, white or color noise addition, multiple bands equalization, echo addition, cropping, quantization, re-sampling, low pass, high pass or band pass filtering. Those attacks can cause watermark detection fail even in changes to the audio signal are subtle and imperceptible. Immunity to attack will remain a challenge, as more types attacks, channels, signal coding and transmission methods are continuously introduced.

Watermarking in the Compressed Domain

The proliferation of the Internet, which has enabled audio material (copyrighted or not) to be disseminated has also make wider the use of all kinds of compressed formats (MP3, AAC, WMA, etc) at a global scale. A good example is the Windows Media Audio (WMA) format from Microsoft, which enables both real time watermarking and audio compression in an effective way. This scheme is used by many online music vendors including Napster. However, once the user downloads the music with the valid key the embedded watermark can be easily removed by some software and infringe on purpose of the audio watermarking. How to develop effective watermarking schemes in the compressed domain will remain an important research area in the future.

REFERENCES

Green, D. M. (1967). Additivity of masking. *The Journal of the Acoustical Society of America*, *41*(6), 1517–1525. doi:10.1121/1.1910514

Humes, L. E., & Jestcart, W. (1989). Models of the additivity of masking. *The Journal of the Acoustical Society of America*, *85*(3), 1285–1294. doi:10.1121/1.397459

Lutfi, R. A. (1983). Additivity of simultaneous masking. *The Journal of the Acoustical Society of America*, *73*(1), 262–267. doi:10.1121/1.388859

Compilation of References

Abbate, A., Decusatis, C. M., & Das, P. K. (2002). *Wavelets and subbands, fundamentals and applications*. Boston, MA: Birkhauser.

Akansu, A., & Smith, M. J. T. (1996). *Subband and wavelet transforms, design and applications*. Norwell, MA: Kluwer Academic Publishers.

Atal, B., & Schroeder, M. R. (1984). Stochastic coding of speech signals at very low bit rates. In *Proceedings of the IEEE International Conference on Communications* (pp. 1610-1613). Amsterdam, Netherlands.

Bas, P., Chassery, J.-M., & Macq, B. (2002). Geometrically invariant watermarking using feature points. *IEEE Transactions on Image Processing, 11*(9), 1014–1028. doi:10.1109/TIP.2002.801587

Bender, W., Gruhl, D., Morimoto, N., & Lu, A. (1996). Techniques for data hiding. *IBM Systems Journal, 35*(3/4), 313–336. doi:10.1147/sj.353.0313

Benedetto, F., Giunta, G., & Neri, A. (2007). QoS assessment of 3G video-phone calls by tracing watermarking exploiting the new colour space 'YST'. *IET Communications, 1*(4), 696–704. doi:10.1049/iet-com:20060331

Bharitkar, S., & Kyriakakis, C. (2006). *Immersive audio signal processing*. New York, NY: Springer. doi:10.1007/0-387-28503-2

Black, M., & Zeytinoglu, M. (1995). Computationally efficient wavelet packet coding of wide-band stereo signals. In *Proceedings of the IEEE International Conference on Acoustics, Speech and Signal Processing (ICASSP)* (pp. 3075-3078). Detroit, MI.

Bosi, M., & Goldberg, R. E. (2003). *Introduction to digital audio coding and standards*. Norwell, MA: Kluwer Academic Publishers.

Cai, L., Tu, R., Zhao, J., & Mao, Y. (2007). Speech quality evaluation: a new application of digital watermarking. *IEEE Transactions on Instrumentation and Measurement, 56*(1), 45–55. doi:10.1109/TIM.2006.887773

Campisi, P., Carli, M., Giunta, G., & Neri, A. (2002). Tracing watermarking for multimedia communication quality assessment. In []. New York, NY.]. *Proceedings of the IEEE International Conference on Communications, 2*, 1154–1158.

Campisi, P., Carli, M., Giunta, G., & Neri, A. (2003). Blind quality assessment system for multimedia communications using tracing watermarking. *IEEE Transactions on Signal Processing, 51*(4), 996–1002. doi:10.1109/TSP.2003.809381

Compilation of References

Carnero, B., & Drygajlo, A. (1999). Perceptual speech coding and enhancement using frame-synchronized fast wavelet packet transform algorithms. *IEEE Transactions on Signal Processing, 47*(6), 1622–1635. doi:10.1109/78.765133

Carnero, B., & Drygajlo, A. (1999). Perceptual speech coding and enhancement using frame-synchronized fast wavelet packet transform algorithms. *IEEE Transactions on Signal Processing, 47*(6), 1622–1635. doi:10.1109/78.765133

Chan, Y. T. (1995). *Wavelet basics.* Norwell, MA: Kluwer Academic Publishers.

Chen, M., He, Y., & Lagendijk, R. L. (2005). A fragile watermark error detection scheme for wireless video communications. *IEEE Transactions on Multimedia, 7*(2), 201–211. doi:10.1109/TMM.2005.843367

Cheng, S., Yu, H., & Xiong, Z. (2002). Enhanced spread spectrum watermarking of MPEG-2 AAC audio. In *Proceedings of the IEEE International Conference on Acoustics, Speech and Signal Processing (ICASSP)* (4, pp. 3728-3731). Orlando, FL.

Chipcenter. (2006). Tutorial on spread spectrum. Retrieved from http://archive.chipcenter.com/ knowledge_centers/digital/ features/ showArticle.jhtml? articleID=9901240

Cox, I. J., Kilian, J., Leighton, T., & Shamoon, T. (1997). Secure spread spectrum watermarking for multimedia. *IEEE Transactions on Image Processing, 6*(12), 1673–1687. doi:10.1109/83.650120

Cox, I. J., Miller, M. L., & Bloom, J. A. (2002). *Digital watermarking.* San Francisco, CA: Academic Press.

Cvejic, N. (2004). *Algorithms for audio watermarking and steganography* (Unpublished doctoral dissertation), University of Oulu, Oulu, Finland. Retrieved from http://herkules. oulu.fi /isbn9514273842/ isbn9514273842. pdf

Cvejic, N., & Seppänen, T. (2003a). Robust audio watermarking in wavelet domain using frequendy hopping and patchwork method. In *Proceedings of the 3rd International Symposium on Image and Signal Processing and Analysis (ISISPA)* (pp. 251-255).

Cvejic, N., & Seppänen, T. (2003b). Fusing digital audio watermarking and authentication in diverse signal domains. In *Proceedings of the European Signal Processing Conference* (pp. 84-87). Antalya, Turkey.

Cvejic, N., Keskinarkaus, A., & Seppänen, T. (2001). Audio watermarking using m-sequences and temporal masking. In *Proceedings of the IEEE ASSP Workshop on Applications of Signal Processing to Audio and Acoustics* (pp. 227-230).

Daubechies, I. (1992). Ten lectures on wavelets. *CBMS-NSF Regional Conference Series in Applied Mathematics, 61.*

Delannay, D., & Macq, B. (2000). Generalized 2D cyclic patterns for secret watermark generation. In []. Vancouver, BC, Canada.]. *Proceedings of the IEEE International Conference of Image Processing, 2,* 72–79.

Deller, J. Hansen, J., & Proakis, J. (1993). *Discrete-time processing of speech signals.* New York, NY: Macmillan Publishing.

Garcia, R. A. (1999). Digital watermarking of audio signals using a psychoacoustic model and spread spectrum theory. In *Proceedings of the 107th Convention of Audio Engineering Society (AES)* (Preprint 5073). New York, NY.

Geiser, B., & Vary, P. (2007). Backwards compatible wideband telephony in mobile networks: CELP watermarking and bandwidth extension. In *Proceedings of the IEEE International Conference on Acoustics, Speech and Signal Processing (ICASSP)* (4, pp. 533-536). Honolulu, HI.

Geiser, B., Jax, P., & Vary, P. (2005). Artificial bandwidth extension of speech supported by watermark-transmitted side information. In *Proceedings of the 9th European Conference on Speech Communication and Technology* (pp. 1497-1500). Lisbon, Portugal.

Gomes, L. de C. T. (2001). Resynchronization methods for audio watermarking. *Proceedings of the 111th Convention of Audio Engineering Society (AES)* (Preprint 5441). New York, NY.

Green, D. M. (1967). Additivity of masking. *The Journal of the Acoustical Society of America, 41*(6), 1517–1525. doi:10.1121/1.1910514

Gruhl, D., Lu, L., & Bender, W. (1996). Echo hiding. In *Proceedings of the Information Hiding Workshop* (pp.295-315). University of Cambridge, UK.

Gür, G., Altug, Y., Anarim, E., & Alagöz, F. (2007). Image error concealment using watermarking with subbands for wireless channels. *IEEE Communications Letters, 11*(2), 179–181. doi:10.1109/LCOMM.2007.061055

Hagmüller, M., & Kubin, G. (2005). *Speech watermarking for air traffic control. EEC Note 05/05.* Eurocontrol Experimental Centre.

He, X., & Scordilis, M. M.(2008-b), Psychoacoustic music analysis based on the discrete wavelet packet transform. *Research Letters in Signal Processing.* doi:10.1155/2008/346767

He, X., & Scordilis, M. M. (2006b). *An Improved spread spectrum digital audio watermarking scheme based on a psychoacoustic model using wavelet packet transform algorithms.* IEEE Transactions on Information Forensics and Security.

He, X., & Scordilis, M. M. (2008a). Efficiently synchronized spread spectrum audio watermarking. *Research Letters in Signal Processing.* doi:10.1155/2008/251868

He, X., & Scordilis, M. M. (2005). Improved spread spectrum digital audio Watermarking Based on Modified Perceptual Entropy Psychoacoustic Model. In *Proceedings of the IEEE Southeast Conference* (pp. 283-286). Miami, FL.

He, X., Iliev, A., & Scordilis, M. M. (2004). A novel high capacity digital audio watermarking system. In *Proceedings of the IEEE International Conference on Acoustics, Speech and Signal Processing (ICASSP)*, (pp. 393-396).

Hellman, R. (1972). Asymmetry of masking between noise and tone. *Perception & Psychophysics, 11*, 241–246. doi:10.3758/BF03206257

Hofbauer, K., Hering, H., & Kübin, G. (2005). Speech watermarking for the VHF radio channel. In *Proceeding of the 4th EUROCONTROL Innovative Research Workshop* (pp. 215-220). Bretigny, France.

Huang, D. Y., & Yeo, T. Y. (2002). Robust and inaudible multi-echo audio watermarking. In *Proceedings of the IEEE Pacific Rim Conference on Multimedia* (pp.615-622). Taiwan, China.

Compilation of References

Huang, X. H. (2009). A complex cepstrum fragile audio watermarking algorithm based on quantization. In *Proceedings of the 3rd International Conference on Genetic and Evolutionary Computing* (pp. 231-234). Guilin, China.

Humes, L. E., & Jestcart, W. (1989). Models of the additivity of masking. *The Journal of the Acoustical Society of America*, *85*(3), 1285–1294. doi:10.1121/1.397459

Jaffard, S., Meyer, Y., & Ryan, R. D. (2001). *Wavelets tools for science and technology.* Philadelphia, PA: SIAM.

Jung, S., Seok, J., & Hong, J. (2003). An improved detection technique for spread spectrum audio watermarking with a spectral envelope filter. *ETRI*, *25*(1), 52–54. doi:10.4218/etrij.03.0203.0103

Kim, H. J. (2003). Audio watermarking techniques. In *Proceedings of the Pacific Rim Workshop on Digital Steganography.* Kitakyushu, Japan.

Kirovski, D., & Malvar, H. S. (2003). Spread-spectrum watermarking of audio signals. *IEEE Transactions on Signal Processing*, *51*(4), 1020–1033. doi:10.1109/TSP.2003.809384

Kirovski, D., & Attias, H. (2002). Audio watermark robustness to de-synchronization via beat detection. In *Proceedings of the 5th International Workshop on Information Hiding* (pp. 160-176). Noordwijkerhout, Netherlands.

Kirovski, D., & Malvar, H. S. (2001). Robust spread-spectrum audio watermarking. In *Proceedings of the IEEE International Conference on Acoustics, Speech and Signal Processing (ICASSP)* (3, pp. 1345-1348). Salt Lake City, UT.

Ko, B. S., Nishimura, R., & Suzuki, Y. (2002). Time-spread echo method for digital audio watermarking using PN sequences. In *Proceedings of the IEEE International Conference on Acoustics, Speech and Signal Processing (ICASSP)* (2, pp. 2001-2004). Orlando, FL.

Kutter, M. (1998). Watermarking resisting to translation, rotation, and scaling. In []. Boston, MA.]. *Proceedings of the SPIE Multimedia Systems and Applications*, *3528*, 423–431.

Li, W., & Xue, X. (2003). An audio watermarking technique that is robust against random cropping. *Computer Music Journal*, *27*(4), 58–68. doi:10.1162/014892603322730505

Lichtenauer, J., Setyawan, I., Kalker, T., & Lagendijk, R. (2003). Exhaustive geometrical search and false positive watermark detection probability. In *Proceedings of the SPIE Electronic Imaging, Security and Watermarking of Multimedia Contents* (4, pp. 203-214). Santa Clara, CA.

Licks, V., & Jordan, R. (2005). Geometric attacks on image watermarking systems. *IEEE MultiMedia*, *12*(3), 68–78. doi:10.1109/MMUL.2005.46

Lin, C., Sow, D., & Chang, S. (2001). Using self-authentication-and-recovery images for error concealment in wireless environments. []. Denver, CO.]. *Proceedings of the Society for Photo-Instrumentation Engineers*, *4518*, 267–274.

Lin, C.-Y., Bloom, J. A., Cox, I. J., Miller, M. L., & Liu, Y. M. (2000). Rotation, scale and translation-resilient public watermarking for images. In *Proceedings of the SPIE Security Watermarking Multimedia Contents II*, *3971*, 90–98.

Lincoln, B. (1998). An experimental high fidelity perceptual audio coder. *Project in MUS420* Retrieved from http://www-ccrma. stanford.edu/ jos/bosse/.

Liu, Q. (2004). *Digital audio watermarking utilizing discrete wavelet packet transform.* (Unpublished Master's thesis). Chaoyang University of Technology, Taiwan, China.

Lutfi, R. A. (1983). Additivity of simultaneous masking. *The Journal of the Acoustical Society of America*, *73*(1), 262–267. doi:10.1121/1.388859

Malvar, H. S., & Florencio, D. A. (2003). Improved spread spectrum: a new modulation technique for robust audio watermarking. *IEEE Transactions on Signal Processing*, *51*(4), 898–905. doi:10.1109/ TSP.2003.809385

Meel Ir. J. (1999). Spread spectrum (SS) introduction, *Denyer Institute Report*. Retrieved from http://www.sss-mag.com /pdf/ Ss_jme_denayer _intro_print.pdf

Oh, H. O., Seok, J. W., Hong, J. W., & Youn, D. H. (2001). New echo embedding technique for robust and imperceptible audio watermarking. In *Proceedings of the IEEE International Conference on Acoustics, Speech and Signal Processing (ICASSP)* (3. pp. 1341-1344). Salt Lake City, UT.

Painter, T., & Spanias, A. (2000). Perceptual coding of digital audio. *Proceedings of the IEEE*, *88*(4), 451–513. doi:10.1109/5.842996

Pan, D. (1995). A tutorial on mpeg/audio compression. *IEEE MultiMedia*, *2*(2), 60–74. doi:10.1109/93.388209

Polikarg, R. (2006). The wavelet tutorial. Retrieved from http://users.rowan.edu/ polikar/ Wavelets/wtpart1.html

Reyes, N. R., Zurera, M. R., Ferreras, F. L., & Amores, P. J. (2003). Adaptive wavelet-packet analysis for audio coding purposes. *Signal Processing*, *83*, 919–929. doi:10.1016/ S0165-1684(02)00489-9

Ruandaidh, J. J. K. O., & Pun, T. (1998). Rotation, scale and translation invariant spread spectrum digital image watermarking. *Signal Processing*, *66*, 303–317. doi:10.1016/ S0165-1684(98)00012-7

Sagi, A., & Malah, D. (2007). Bandwidth extension of telephone speech aided by data embedding. *EURASIP Journal on Advances in Signal Processing*. doi:10.1155/2007/64921

Sajatovic, M., Prinz, J., & Kroepfl, A. (2003). Increasing the safety of the ATC voice communications by using in-band messaging. In *Proceedings of the 22nd Digital Avionics Systems Conference* (1, pp. 4.E.1-1-8). Indianapolis, IN.

Scharf, B. (1970). Critical Bands. In Tobia, J. V. (Ed.), *Foundations of modern auditory theory,* (1, pp. 157-202). New York, NY: Academic Press.

Seok, J., Hong, J., & Kim, J. (2002). A novel audio watermarking algorithm for copyright protection of digital audio. *ETRI Journal*, *24*(3), 181–189. doi:10.4218/ etrij.02.0102.0301

Sinha, D., & Tewfik, A. (1993). Low bit rate transparent audio compression using adapted wavelets. *IEEE Transactions on Signal Processing*, *41*(12), 3463–3479. doi:10.1109/78.258086

Spanias, A., Painter, T., & Atti, V. (2007). *Audio signal processing and coding.* Hoboken, NJ: Wiley-Interscience Press. doi:10.1002/0470041978

Compilation of References

Swanson, M. D., Zhu, B., Tewfik, A. H., & Boney, L. (1998). Robust audio watermarking using perceptual masking. *Elsevier Signal Processing, Special Issue on Copyright Protection and Access Control, 66*(3), 337–355.

Tzanetakis, G., Essl, G., & Cook, P. (2001). Audio analysis using the discrete wavelet transforms. In *Proceedings of the International Conference of Acoustics and Music: Theory and Applications.* Skiathos, Greece. Retrieved from http://www.cs.princeton.edu/~gessl/papers/amta2001.pdf.

Vaseghi, S. V. (2000). *Advanced digital signal processing and noise reduction.* Hoboken, NJ: John Wiley & Sons, Ltd.

Veldhuis, R. N. J., Breeuwer, M., & Van Der Wall, R. G. (1989). Subband coding of digital audio signals. *Philips Journal of Research, 44*(2/3), 329–343.

Wikipedia (2009). Retrieved from http://en.wikipedia.org/wiki/Ear

William, H. P., Saul, A. T., William, T. V., & Brian, P. F. (1992). *Numerical Recipes in C.* Cambridge, UK: Cambridge University Press.

Wu, S., Huang, J., Huang, D., & Shi, Y. Q. (2005). Efficiently self-synchronized audio watermarking for assured audio data transmission. *IEEE Transactions on Broadcasting, 51*(1), 69–76. doi:10.1109/TBC.2004.838265

Wu, C.-P., Su, P.-C., & Kuo, C.-C. J. (1999). Robust audio watermarking for copyright protection. *Proceedings of the Society for Photo-Instrumentation Engineers, 3807,* 387–397.

Wu, C.-P., Su, P.-C., & Kuo, C.-C. J. (2000). Robust and efficient digital audio watermarking using audio content analysis. *Proceedings of the Society for Photo-Instrumentation Engineers, 3971,* 382–392.

Xu, C., Wu, J., Sun, Q., & Xin, K. (1999). Applications of digital watermarking technology in audio signals. *Journal of the Audio Engineering Society. Audio Engineering Society, 47*(10), 805–812.

Zurera, M. R., Ferreras, F. L., Amores, M. P. J., Bascon, S. M., & Reyes, N. R. (2001). A new algorithm for translating psychoacoustic information to the wavelet domain. *Signal Processing, 81,* 519–531. doi:10.1016/S0165-1684(00)00230-9

Zurera, M. R., Ferreras, F. L., Amores, M. P. J., Bascon, S. M., & Reyes, N. R. (2001). A new algorithm for translating psychoacoustic information to the wavelet domain. *Signal Processing, 81,* 519–531. doi:10.1016/S0165-1684(00)00230-9

Zwicker, E., & Fastl, H. (1990). *Psychoacoustics Facts and Models.* New York, NY: Springer-Verlag.

Zwicker, E., & Zwicker, U. (1991). Audio engineering and psychoacoustics: matching signals to the final receiver, the human auditory system. *Journal of the Audio Engineering Society. Audio Engineering Society, 39,* 115–126.

About the Author

Xing He is a senior audio research engineer in the research group at SRS Labs. Inc. located in Santa Ana, California. From January 2006 to August 2008, he was a principal systems engineer in the research group at BrainMedia, LLC located in New York City. Prior to this appointment, he was a research engineer at the Panasonic (China) Research and Development Center conducting research on Automatic Speech Recognition (ASR). He holds a PhD from the Department of Electrical and Computer Engineering at the University of Miami, in addition to his master's and bachelor's degrees from the Department of Electrical Engineering at Beijing Jiaotong University, Beijing, China. Dr. He's research focuses on digital signal processing, with emphasis on speech signal enhancement, perceptual audio coding and compression, psychoacoustic modeling, and digital audio watermarking.

Index